Beautiful
PLACES, SPIRITUAL
Spaces

Beautiful
PLACES, SPIRITUAL
Spaces

SHARON HANBY-ROBIE
& DEB STRUBEL

NORTHFIELD®
PUBLISHING

All Scripture quotations, unless otherwise indicated, are
taken from the *Holy Bible, New International Version*®. NIV®.
Copyright © 1973, 1978, 1984 by International Bible Society. Used by permission of Zondervan Publishing House.
All rights reserved.

Scripture quotations marked NKJV are taken from the *New
King James Version*. Copyright © 1982, 1992 by Thomas Nelson, Inc. Used by permission. All rights reserved.

Scripture quotations marked KJV are taken from the King
James Version.

Library of Congress Cataloging-in-Publication Data

Hanby-Robie, Sharon.
  Beautiful places, spiritual spaces: the art of stress-free
interior design / Sharon Hanby-Robie and Deb Strubel.
      p. cm
   ISBN 1-881273-18-0
   1. Christian women—Religious life. 2. Home—Religious
aspects—Christianity. 3. Interior decoration. I. Strubel,
Deborah. II. Title
   BV4527.H355 2004
   248.8′43—dc22

                                      2004006202

1 3 5 7 9 10 8 6 4 2
Printed in the United States of America

To God for His inspiration, kindness, and blessing, to my husband and my mother for their continued encouragement and faith in me, and to my clients, who have allowed me the pleasure of working with them in their homes.
—Sharon

To my husband who puts up with my piles and to my parents who taught me the value of a kitchen junk drawer.
—Deb

Contents

Introduction

PSALM 133:1 NKJV

"Behold, how good and how pleasant it is for brethren to dwell together in unity!"

When I think about "home sweet home," images from my childhood come to mind—fluffy feather pillows, the wooden toy chest, the tire swing in the backyard. We adults still want our homes to feel carefree, peaceful, and safe. We want them to be full of hugs and laughter.

What feelings come to mind when you think about your home today?

It's wonderful to have a beautifully decorated home as long as you are not a slave to it. A beautiful home is only a blessing if it meets your needs, rather than you having to slave to meet its needs.

Too often our dream of an ideal home is unrealistic. What should matter the most is having a home that gives you, your family, and your friends the freedom to be yourselves. It should meet the *needs* of the family.

As an interior designer, I (Sharon) have spent my life working with real people and real families in their most personal and cherished spaces—their homes. Our homes should be the places where we have the freedom to relax and express ourselves. At the same time, as Christian women we know that God wants us to have a positive influence on those around us. We want to use our homes to nurture our families and friendships, new and old. We want a home that looks beautiful, is easy to maintain, and meets our needs.

Finding balance between the spiritual and the physical needs within the home is key to creating an atmosphere of love. Creating a nurturing environment for our children and visitors is important. A home is where we "come from." It is our foundation. Our homes are the first worlds that our children know. Here they gain their first impressions of what to expect from the world. Our homes determine how they look at and treat outsiders and will influence the rest of their lives. As Florence Littauer said, "It's not the surroundings but the spirit that makes for genuine hospitality."[1]

We must nurture our spiritual centers since the Spirit is such an important part of us and of our homes. That's why Deb and I have taken a unique approach in this book. We've integrated spiritual insights and questions with solid design advice.

You may use this book anyway you like, but here's one idea. On Sunday, or the day you have the most time, read the opening Scripture and the sentence under "Day 1." Each day of that week reread the verse and read the next day's thought or question. The sentence meditations will focus your first thoughts, but it will be amazing to see how God leads your mind. If you miss a day, don't worry. You can easily read several meditations at once. We made them short because we know you are busy.

Anytime during the week, read the accompanying design lesson. Be sure to catch the practical design tips at the end of each unit. Then enjoy implementing the spiritual insights and design tips into your life and home as you nurture yourself and your loved ones.

NOTES

1. Florence Littauer, *It Takes So Little To Be Above Average* (Eugene, Oreg.: Harvest House, 1996).

Meditations on Firm Foundations

ISAIAH 33:6

"He (God) will be the sure foundation for your times,
a rich store of salvation and wisdom and knowledge;
the fear of the LORD is the key to this treasure."

Day 1
Thank You, God, for Your promise of a sure foundation even though
sometimes I feel shaky.

Day 2
What are the "rich stores" on which my life and my home are built?

Day 3
Thank You for granting me salvation and wisdom and knowledge.

Day 4
How can I properly fear You?

Day 5
Teach me how to anchor my home on Your foundation.

Day 6
Grant my loved ones and me a renewed sense of our treasure in You.

See photo #2

Firm Foundations

A home is an earthly foundation. As children, it is the first environment we know, and from it we learn what to expect from family and outsiders. Our home lives will determine how we look at and approach the rest of the world and the rest of our lives.

In her book *Your Life,* Nancy Carmichael said: "It is one thing to have a wonderfully decorated and furnished house; but is the house for you, or do you exist for the house? We have real fellowship when we feel safe with one another, when there is earned trust in the relationship. Fellowship is for us, the real people with real needs. There is nothing sweeter than authentic relationships."

THE BASIS FOR SOCIETY

All aspects of our lives are touched and affected by the atmosphere of our homes. One of the most important things that we can do is to establish a home that is joyful, comfortable, and encouraging to those who dwell there.

Home life shapes families and societies. Architecturally, a well-designed and well-constructed home is one of the finer accomplishments of humankind. But a home is more than bricks and mortar. It is a place where family members can receive physical, emotional, and spiritual nourishment. As Franklin Delano Roosevelt said, "Safe, affordable housing is a basic necessity for every family. Without a decent place to live, people cannot be productive members of society, children cannot learn and families cannot thrive."

Our homes should not only reflect our personal tastes but also express the personalities of all those who live there. Personal mementos and heirlooms passed down through the family can make a house feel like a home.

Most people stop short of finishing their homes. They get the major pieces of furniture and maybe an accessory or two. But that is just the foundation. It is the little things—color, texture, pattern, wallcoverings, area rugs, pillows, a soft throw, plants, artwork, and treasures collected throughout your life—that truly make the difference.

BEGIN WITH LOVE

One of the most frequent questions I (Sharon) hear is "Where do I begin?"

Start with something you love. Whether it's a piece of artwork, a rug, a lamp, a chair, or even a piece of wallpaper, it doesn't matter as long as you love it. Then build the space around that treasured item. Learn to collect things. The objects we collect tell stories and hold memories. Finding and living with objects that we love can bring joy.

The secret is to make choices that are right for you and your family. Arrange or rearrange in a way that makes life simpler and easier. If your children hear the words "no" and "don't" every time they enter or use a room, it means your home rules are overruling practical living, and there is something wrong with the choices you have made. As Carole Mayhall says, "Being a keeper of the home is a big task, but it won't be overwhelming if you keep trying to simplify your home as well as your life."[1]

Here are some tips for improving the foundation of your home life:

- Allow your home to be a living home that adapts to meet the changing needs and lifestyles.

- Evaluate your space and needs. Prioritize the tasks that need to be addressed in each room. If you expect children to do homework in the family room, then provide them with a table or desk.

- Don't let the fashion of the moment dictate your spaces, because you will end up sacrificing function and personal taste, which will directly impact your enjoyment of life.

- Make room for fun. Create safe spaces where children can be themselves.

- Be respectful of each family member's privacy and personal possessions.

- Designate a place or room as the "listening space." As a child, my family's spot was the kitchen table. We gathered there to express our feelings, converse with each other, and gain acceptance and recognition.

NOTE

1. Carole Mayhall, *Come Walk with Me* (Colorado Springs: WaterBrook, 1998), 31.

Meditations on Being a Woman of Influence

PROVERBS 14:1

"A wise woman builds her house, but with her own hands the foolish one tears hers down."

Day 1
Lord, show me the foolish things I do that tear down my house and alienate my family.

Day 2
Forgive me for doing things that hurt those I love.

Day 3
What can I do today to "build" my house?

Day 4
Help me to be more self-controlled and patient at home.

Day 5
What attitudes do I need to build into my life so that I may better nurture my family and friends?

Day 6
Teach me Your wisdom.

Being a Woman of Influence

Proverbs 14:1 is one of my favorite verses. I am awed at how much influence women have within their homes. We set the tone and the atmosphere, and that impacts the lives of all who enter. What a responsibility! What an opportunity! As Christians, we have such an advantage—the Lord is the giver of wisdom! By following His example we can be sure that we are building homes that will comfort and nourish both body and soul.

Someone defined comfort as a sense of contentment we find in a place that "feels like home." That definition is interesting because our earthly homes are only temporary. They can only *feel* like home, since heaven is our eternal home. In the meantime, we can do our best to make our homes places that bring comfort.

COMFORTS OF HOME

Country Living magazine invited readers to share what brought them comfort in their homes. The answers were as unique as the individuals writing. For some, it was baking bread or the sound of the family dog snoring softly at the foot of the bed. Another woman cherished the routine of sharing a cup of coffee with her best friend every day at 5 P.M. Deb loves to lie in bed listening to the sound of small planes taking off and approaching the small airport near her home.

Home isn't just a building. A home is a project in process. It helps to stop occasionally and ask ourselves how we are doing at building our homes. Do we treat our family members with the same respect and civility with which we treat others? Listen to the noises in your home. Are they generally happy sounds? Are your words and tone gentle? Are you fostering an attitude of joy in togetherness? Little things like sharing the weekend chores bring a family together and make a house feel like home.

TO HOME AND BEYOND

Another important element of building our homes is our relationship with God. The wise woman depends on God for her daily strength. Of course, eating right, exercising, and getting enough rest all help too. But a woman of godly character is so attractive in spirit that others can't help but be drawn to her presence.

From time to time, Deni and her husband, a high school teacher, invited his students to breakfast and Bible study in their home. "They made me feel very welcomed and loved," said Jon, a former student. "They were real and down-to-earth, and that let me be real and open with them. When I think back on my growing-up years, they stick out as two people who God used to shape and challenge me."

A wise woman does things to nurture herself, her spouse, and her children. In so doing she will nurture others in her wider circle of influence.

We all need a place to call home, a place in this world that we can truly call our sanctuary. As one writer said, home is the place where cares can be traded for dreams and where every moment spent is sweet, strengthening, and good for the soul.

Here are some ideas for making your house a home that your family loves:

- Instead of worrying about decorating, surround yourself with things you love, perhaps a cozy shawl or throw over the arm of your favorite chair.

- Incorporate family heirlooms into each room.

- Improve your health by arranging furniture so you can sit and see out the window. It takes only ten minutes of looking at God's green earth to lower your blood pressure.

- Use fabrics to transform your home into a cohesive comfort zone. Flow a unifying color into every room, and your treasures will easily work together.

- By blending colors, fabrics, and rugs from room to room, you can create the illusion of more space.

- Bake an apple pie or something else that smells and tastes pleasant, and then grab a corner of the couch and read a book to yourself or your children.

Meditations on Designing a Peaceful Place

ISAIAH 32:18

*"My people will live in peaceful dwelling places,
in secure homes, in undisturbed places of rest."*

Day 1
What do I envision when I hear the word *peace?*

Day 2
What do my family members envision as a peaceful setting?

Day 3
Thank You, Lord, for calling me one of Your people and for Your promise
to provide a peaceful dwelling place.

Day 4
Thank You that my ultimate security rests in You.

Day 5
When I lie down to sleep, quiet my racing thoughts and slow
my pounding heart.

Day 6
O Lord, how I long for a place of unending peace. May my home become
a haven of peace and undisturbed rest.

Designing a Peaceful Place

When it comes to creating an atmosphere of peace and harmony, we probably don't think of color first. Yet color is all around us. Whether we are aware of its effect on us or not, it plays a vital role in how we live. Color can influence our thinking, feelings, and actions. It can irritate or calm our spirits, raise our blood pressure, and even make us hungry!

CLUE IN TO COLOR

Scientists, artists, and musicians have studied color for centuries, searching for a way to explain its influence on man and animals. They have approached the concept of color from physiological, philosophical, and artistic perspectives. Although there are many different theories, there is rarely a consensus.

Why? Color is specific to the individual who sees it. How we react to a color is the result of a combination of our education, our history of exposure to it, our culture, and our eye's physical ability to see it. There are, of course, some examples where most people agree. For example, blue makes most people feel cool. No, not like "Hey, I'm cool!" but temperature cool, like "I feel chilly."

Choosing the right color for your home is probably the hardest decorating decision you have to make. It's also far more important than most of us realize, because color affects us in so many ways, consciously and subconsciously. Children are sensitive to color as well. We can actually make them feel better about themselves and their spaces by the right color choices. (See pages 63–64 under the heading "Use a Signature Print" for more on children and colors.)

SATISFY YOURSELF AND YOUR FAMILY

Decorate your home with the colors you and your family love. It doesn't matter what the latest trends are or what the fashion gurus think. What *does* matter is that you love your home and that your choices make sense for you and your family. One man I know is color-blind. For years, his wife graciously allowed him to choose the wall color for his den and a few additional rooms. He said those rooms were the only places that looked good to him, but he and his color-blind friends were the only ones who called them attractive.

The use of color is an easy and inexpensive way to bring a little peace and harmony to your home. Try using calming colors of green, lilac, or blue in the areas where you relax as a family or in your bedrooms. At the end of a day, add some quiet inspirational background music and you will bring a bit of heaven into your atmosphere, which should be good for the soul!

Nature is a major influential force for our color choices. Blue is one of the most dominant colors of the decade, but orange is the hue of choice as a symbol of optimism and happiness. Here are some ways to use color to influence your mood. Your feelings about a particular color may be different based on your background and experience, so don't feel abnormal if you don't fit the norm.

Here are some general tips on color:

- To make a space feel cooler, use cool colors such as blues, violets, or greens.

- To make a space feel warmer, use warm colors such as reds, oranges, or yellows.

- If your family tends to overeat, try painting the kitchen and dining room blue. Cool colors tend to diminish appetites.

- Coral, soft teal, sage, or even a monochromatic tone-on-tone palette can make you feel calm and serene.

- Overall, strive for colors that are fresh and clean.

- An ambiguous hue is a good choice when trying to blend a series of colors. For example, a shade of burgundy could look red or purple. Historical colors fall into the ambiguous range and are popular because they fit with many schemes.

Meditations on Blue and Green People

REVELATION 4:2-3, 6

"At once I was in the Spirit, and there before me was a throne in heaven with someone sitting on it. And the one who sat there had the appearance of jasper and carnelian. A rainbow, resembling an emerald, encircled [God's] throne. . . . Also before the throne there was what looked like a sea of glass, clear as crystal."

Day 1
God loves colors, from the clear, diamondlike jasper to the red of carnelian to the green of emerald to the crystal blue of a sea of glass.

Day 2
Thousands of years ago God invented the rainbow as a symbol of His grace and mercy—and He made it in all colors. I pray to appreciate every color, even those I don't normally like.

Day 3
The Hebrew word for *rainbow* has the sense of bending, as in a bow and arrow. Next time I see a rainbow, let me think of it as God bending His mercy around the earth.

Day 4
Do I need to bend my will for someone in my family to show them I love them?

Day 5
How can I be more inclusive, more loving toward those who have differing opinions?

Day 6
Is God a green or a blue person? Perhaps He's both. Praise God. He filled the earth with colors for everyone.

Blue and Green People

The world is divided into two groups of people: blue and green. I have found that these two colors evoke the strongest emotional response in everyone. In fact, about 33 percent of the population loves green. I call these the green people. The others love blue. You guessed it; these are the blue people.

Most men are blue people. Scientists have discovered that men's brains operate differently with regard to color. Men see fewer colors than women do. Of course, with all theories, there are exceptions to the rule. If a man turns out to be a green person, he is always involved in a creative field.

My blue/green theory does not exclude other colors. You may not even use blue or green in your decorating scheme. My theory is just an easy way to determine the basis of your choices. It's also one explanation why you and your spouse or family members may have trouble agreeing on a home color scheme.

TAKE A FUN TEST

Over the years I have discovered that most people can tell me what they *don't* like, but not what they *do* like. As a result I have developed a little test—Sharon's Creative Color Test—that will help you determine the right colors, patterns, and styles, and the level of formality that is right for you. Think of it like a psychologist's inkblot test.

Rather than using ink splotches, I use fabric swatches. You could use wallpaper books, paint chips, or flooring samples. The point of the test is to go through lots of swatches and respond from your heart. Don't analyze or think about where you might use a particular fabric; simply choose those patterns, textures, or colors that make you smile. Once you have established a "yes" pile of samples, go back and evaluate them.

DO YOU LIKE BOLD OR CALM?

What are the three main colors you chose? Are they bold and dramatic or simply tone-on-tone monochromatic color choices? These choices indicate the colors that are right for you. Green people also tend to like brighter, more adventurous tones such as purple, red, teal, and hot pink. Blue people usually tend to be happier with peach, mauve, gray, beige, or brown tones.

If you are a blue person, then the shades of green that appeal to you will have blue undertones. It is possible for blue and green people to like the same patterns, but in different color combinations. For the most part, blue people prefer calmer, less radical patterns. Green people often like things with more zing! An example of a "true blue" color combination is yellow, blue, orange and white, as in Portuguese china. A "true green" color combo is green, red, cream, and white.

Recently while working with a couple, the woman chose a beautiful red-toned pattern for chairs. Her husband chose a beige ground pattern that nearly blended into the carpet. He said he felt overwhelmed with the red. To keep both of them happy, we compromised with a deep blue stripe that incorporated a rich woven tapestry of orange, gold, red, and green that was placed between the stripes. They loved it!

In the nearly thirty years I have been using this test with clients, I have discovered an amazing secret: The choices you make will consistently hold true for your lifetime because you are who you are, and you are not suddenly going to wake up tomorrow and be someone else. The colors, pattern styles, and textures that you have a positive emotional response to will always appeal to you. So go ahead—trust your instincts.

Here are some tips for taking Sharon's Creative Color Test:

- Don't second-guess yourself or spend time studying the samples. Put the "Yes, I like that . . . I'm not sure for where, but I like it" patterns in the "yes" stack. Put the "Well, I don't know. Maybe. Maybe not" in the "no" pile.

- Be sure to include test samples of styles, colors, and patterns that you normally avoid. This will give you a chance to consider new ideas.

- When you are finished compiling your "yes" pile, begin the analysis. Are the samples dominantly blue or green? Are the colors you chose bright or soft? Are they strong or subtle in feeling? This will tell a lot about your personal style.

- It is important to keep the hue or shade (strength or paleness) of the colors in balance. A really strong red will not balance with a very pale yellow. When decorating, the intensity of each color must be at the same level.

- Color affects the scale of items. For example, a chair covered in a bright or dark color will appear heavier or larger than if it was covered in a light color.

Meditations on Patterns of Living

2 TIMOTHY 1:13

"What you have heard from me, keep as the pattern of sound teaching, with faith and love in Christ Jesus."

Day 1
Thank You, Lord, for the pattern of sound teaching that I have received—whether it is from Your Word, my family, my church, or my godly friends.

Day 2
Let me hold fast to the gospel I have been taught.

Day 3
Help me continue to listen and watch for good patterns to imitate, just as Paul, the writer of this verse, was a prototype for Timothy.

Day 4
How can I exhibit love as I live?

Day 5
May I not just keep to what I have been taught, but may I expand and grow in faith and love.

Day 6
Can my loved ones point to my life as a good pattern of godly living?

Patterns of Living

Just as God's pattern can set the tone of our lives, color and pattern can set the mood of a room. Bold stripes, for instance, look great in a contemporary space, while tiny floral patterns fit better in a casual, country-style home. Silks, brocades, and damask patterns set a formal mood. Our homes should be a reflection of our personalities, and skillful use of patterns is one of the best ways to communicate who we are.

SAFE EQUALS BORING

Unfortunately, when it comes to patterns, many people lack the confidence to use them. Why? Because most people don't know the rules for mixing and matching patterns. Rather than make a mistake, they choose to keep things simple, which can be boring!

If you took my Creative Color Test (page 26), look at the swatches in your "yes" pile. If you no longer have them, take the test again. When you are finished, analyze the types of patterns you chose. Are there delicate florals or small stripes or plaids? Are there dramatic prints or exotic textures? These choices indicate the patterns that are right for you.

Are your choices formal or informal? Contemporary or traditional? Perhaps you have a bit of both. If so, then a transitional design is best for you.

Are your samples busy or simple? Knowing this will give you further insight to your personal taste. I prefer cleaner lines. As I've *matured* (I hate that word!), I have acquired a taste for more details—hence, my preference for French country style, which has more intricate patterns and ornate designs.

COMBINE WITH CONFIDENCE

If you find you have chosen formal style fabrics such as damask or brocade, yet formal would not be appropriate for your current lifestyle, then use the formal fabrics sparingly. For example, choose a formal fabric as an accent only for pillows, drapery trim, table runners, or a throw. That way, you combine the beauty of formal, rich fabrics with the practicality of other simpler, potentially washable, fabrics.

Complement the patterns you have chosen with "broken" color or textures such as glazes, patinas, antique gold or distressing, or verdigris finishes for a unique style with depth of character. By repeating materials, forms, or scale you will lend harmony to a space.

Ella Church Rodman said, "There is no reason, either in prose or in rhyme, why a whole house should not be a poem." I think a home should be a poem that reflects our lives and our loves.

Here are some additional tips to help you coordinate your home like a pro:

> ✎ When mixing fabric patterns and colors, remember the interior designer's rule of three:
>
> 1. Your color palette should have three colors: a main, a contrasting, and an accent. Use the accent color in three different places within the room.

2. Choose three patterns with three different scales, for example, a large floral, a medium plaid, and a small print. Several patterns in the same scale will visually compete with one another.

3. To maintain balance, the main fabric ought to make up two-thirds of what is used, the second fabric is one-third of what is used, and the third fabric is used to accent. For example, if the Creative Color Test indicated that you prefer tiny prints, you should make a small print your main fabric and use a bolder pattern for your accents.

ନ୍ଧ To make a room appear larger, repeat the same pattern throughout, even on the ceiling and furniture.

ନ୍ଧ If using two different wallpaper patterns on one wall, place the darker, optically heavier pattern on the bottom. I often use paper above a chair rail and choose the darker background color for painting below the chair rail.

ନ୍ଧ Make sure all patterns have the same neutral as a background. In other words, don't mix a warm, cream background pattern with a pure white or gray background pattern.

ନ୍ଧ Remember to consider the overall effect of the pattern. For example, a chair covered in a bright or dark pattern will appear heavier or larger than if it was covered in a light pattern.

Meditations on Making an Entrance

PSALM 100:4

"Enter his gates with thanksgiving and his courts with praise; give thanks to him and praise his name."

Day 1
Do others enter my door with thanksgiving?

Day 2
Do I enter my house with thanksgiving? Or do I come home full of frustration and gripes?

Day 3
Lord, forgive me for being ungrateful.

Day 4
Put a song of praise for You in my heart and on my lips.

Day 5
Let my joy for You overflow as I remember Your faithfulness to all generations.

Day 6
What can I do to spruce up my door or entryway so my home looks more inviting and joyful?

Making an Entrance

Have you ever really thought about entering the gates of heaven? I often wonder what the doorway to heaven will look like. What will I see when I first enter? Most importantly, what will I say to our awesome God? I'm a chatterbox, but I imagine I will be speechless in His presence—which is probably a good thing, because I am sure if I spoke, I would embarrass myself with words not fit for my King. In addition, shouldn't we at all times be in step with His Spirit, who lives in us? Shouldn't the atmosphere of our homes, too, be reflective of the Holy Spirit?

If our eyes are the windows to the soul, then a home's entryway is the window to the heart of the home. It is the first impression—the feeling, appearance, and condition of our door or entryway—that will tell everyone what to expect inside. When was the last time you actually entered your home through the front door? Try it. You may be surprised at what you see. In most cases, a little paint, some sweeping of the front stoop, some plants, flowers, and a welcoming wreath could make a world of difference.

Once inside, the front foyer can be a prelude to the entire home. In a way, it is the stage set of our home. It is one of the few spaces where we can allow ourselves the freedom to be dramatic in our decorating choices, because it is a "pass-through" room.

JUST PASSING THROUGH

A pass-through space is one in which we don't

spend a lot of time; we just pass through. Powder rooms and hallways are also considered pass-through spaces, as are staircases.

We can be bolder in our choices in these spaces since we will not be subjected to them for extended periods of time. Don't get me wrong. I don't mean you should be gaudy in your choices, but allow yourself to move beyond your normal comfort level. It's an opportunity to show your colors! And it is one of the easiest places to live with wallcoverings. Large-scale floral or vine patterns work beautifully to open up and fill a foyer with color and life. Floral patterns help unify a color palette.

NOT SO GLAD TO SEE YOU

What kind of mood are you in when you first get home at the end of a day? Too often we enter our homes in a miserable mood. If the first thing I see when I walk into my home is clutter, it can set me off. I try to exercise self-control, and over the years I have gotten better.

My clients frequently mention similar complaints. Many of the things that we argue about, or are frustrated by, can easily be eliminated with little changes in the way our homes function. For example, something as simple as where we drop our keys, handbag, shoes, and books can clean up clutter and make daily maintenance much easier by eliminating the need to nag the kids and spouse. Creating a home that you can enter with thanksgiving can be that simple.

Here are some ideas to help you and your entryway gain a whole new perspective and look:

⚬ The next time you are dashing through your entry, slow down. Pretend for a moment that you are a guest seeing this space for the first time. How does it feel?

⚬ If your foyer is dark and short on natural light, supplement it by adding ceiling, table, or floor lamps. It's amazing what a little light can do.

⚬ Analyze your traffic patterns. Do you enter through the front door, back door, or garage? Plan an organized shoes, keys, and bag drop-off system for everyone. For example, if you take your shoes off the minute you come home, then design a place at the door to leave your shoes and retrieve your slippers.

Meditations on Living in the Great Room

DEUTERONOMY 31:12

"Assemble the people—men, women and children, and the aliens living in your towns—so they can listen and learn to fear the LORD your God and follow carefully all the words of this law."

Day 1
When I think of assembling to learn of God, I think of going to church. Yet my family room is a place where people congregate. What do they discover about God in my home?

Day 2
Do I model a Christlike life?

Day 3
Do I listen to You, Lord—I mean *really* listen?

Day 4
Teach me the proper fear or awe of You.

Day 5
May my home be a place where family and friends love to assemble.

Day 6
Grant that my household and I all choose to serve You.

See photo #5

Living in the Great Room

Homes are forever evolving. Today more than ever, I am seeing sensible changes that make homes most suited for real living. Thankfully, we have realized that family is more important than formal, museum rooms. Today's homes have great rooms, family rooms, and living rooms that we actually live in. And guess what the latest trend is? Rec rooms! Yes, the old-fashioned recreation room is back. I think this is a good sign, a sign that family life is once again a central focus.

I am currently working with several clients who have made the decision to convert their small family rooms. What used to be next to the kitchen is becoming an extension of the kitchen—more of a keeping room or gathering space. A *new* family room is made in what was the *living room.* These people are smart to find areas of their homes that are not frequently used and convert those spaces into areas they can really live in. Additionally, I have several clients with young children who are converting their basements into recreation spaces for playing, skating, bicycle riding, and other active fun!

PLANNING FOR SANITY

It's a blessing to have a space where playmates and neighbors feel free to congregate. Such a home must be free of "do not touch" signs—invisible or otherwise. Planning a family room is crucial since this is where the family will spend most of its time together. One key element is choosing the right rugged furniture, fabrics, and other finishes. Today's new fabrics make it easy to have a simple, clean, and elegant look without fuss. Polyester fabrics that look like suede can be sponged clean, as can faux leathers. Washable slipcovers are a great choice as well. Simplicity is important; use few accessories or knick-knacks to keep clutter to a minimum.

Flexibility combined with multifunction is a great way to successful living space. Storage ottomans have become a mainstay in most of the family rooms I have designed, providing storage for games and magazines as well as additional seating. They can also be used as a coffee table by placing a serving tray on top. Of course, as intended, they're still the perfect resting place for tired feet and legs after chasing the little ones.

PLANNING FOR HARMONY

Consider both adults and children when making decisions about the family room since it is a place where everyone ought to feel comfortable. Bold colors, patterns, and intriguing lines add pizzazz. Or you can choose a simple color palette such as neutral gold or sunny yellow, which creates a warm, glowing room. Comfortable seating that accommodates all ages and heartfelt personal touches will draw family and friends together in a space like this. I always try to include a game table since games bring generations together.

Family rooms are for television viewing and movie watching, so place the TV in a spot that makes sense rather than trying to cram it into a corner. I put the TV on the same wall as the fireplace if possible. If not, plan your furniture—swivel chairs, for example—and its arrangement so that viewing either the fire or the TV can be done easily.

Here are some thoughts for planning your family's living space:

- Consider the ages of your children. Their needs and yours will change through the years. Toddlers like to play within sight and sound of parents, but teens want privacy and invisible parents.

- Do you have pets? What color are they? Never purchase a dark colored sofa if you have a white dog or cat!

- Is the room sunny or dark? Choose colors that will work to make the best of this space. Warm a cool room with sunny colors. Allow daylight to brighten a dark room through open window treatments.

- How organized are you? How organized do you want to be? Plan for easy storage. Life is so much better with a room that can be uncluttered easily. Baskets, shelves, and cupboards are simple ways for making a space easy to clean and organize.

- Do you read, knit, or craft in this space? If so, be sure to include task lighting that adapts to each hobby. I prefer a floor lamp with two adjustable arms for dual use.

Meditations on Fabulous Focal Points

PHILIPPIANS 3:13–14

"One thing I do: Forgetting what is behind and straining toward what is ahead, I press on toward the goal to win the prize for which God has called me heavenward in Christ Jesus."

Day 1
I deal with so many details each day that I can easily lose my focus about what is truly important.

Day 2
Where is my focus?

Day 3
Forgive me, Lord, for my lack of focus on You and the important things of life, like my friends and family members.

Day 4
Help me press on toward the goal of living out Christ's purposes for me—to draw others and myself nearer to Him every day, until I am called home to heaven.

Day 5
Does my home lack focus on You? How can I live so that my loved ones know that my life and my home are centered on You?

Day 6
Where should I focus my energies today?

See photo #7

Fabulous Focal Points

You should be able to walk into any room and be drawn to something beautiful or architecturally powerful. The thing your eye is immediately drawn to when you enter a room is called the focal point. A focal point organizes a room, making sense out of what could be chaos. A focal point can be anything from a piece of artwork or a quilt to a fireplace mantel.

When creating a focal point, think about the room's uses. Some uses seem simple. For example, you expect to sleep in your bedroom, so the bed is the natural focal point, but you may also want to watch television, read, exercise, work on your computer, or iron. (Yes, for some strange reason, this has become a favorite place to keep an ironing board!) If you use an armoire or wall system to house these items, you could make that the focal point.

CONSIDER THE FLOOR PLAN

Furniture should be arranged around your focal point. If you have a fireplace, arrange the furniture to draw the eye to it. Make a list of what you will be using each room for, and then determine each room's floor plan to provide the best environment for those activities. This list helps you decide which pieces of furniture are most important and where they ought to be placed.

Although the floor plan is the most important part of the design process, sometimes the most functional layout is not necessarily the most visually satisfying. Take heart! With the proper selection of colors and textures, almost any plan can be made attractive. The key to a good floor plan is balance. There are two kinds of balance: *physical* and *optical.* In other words, you want to be sure that the arrangement of high and low furniture, combined with the high and low architectural elements (windows, doors, fireplace) is balanced. You don't want your furniture to look like railroad cars, all lined up with no place to go.

Start by placing your largest or most important piece of furniture first. Often there is only one place that a large piece can fit. If so, work from that point. The remaining pieces of furniture should be placed according to their respective sizes with the smallest pieces being positioned last.

Here are some suggestions for creating the perfect plan for your room's focal point:

⊙ Evaluate your room for a built-in focal point. A fireplace or even a spectacular view can be the focus.

⊙ If there is no built-in architectural focal point, then you must choose an item or plan an area of the room to be the center of attention. This can be a conversation area, an entertainment area, the bed in the bedroom, or even a high piece of furniture such as an armoire.

⊙ Once you determine the focal point, establish placement of the larger and more important items in the room around the focal view. The focal point is an object within the room. The focal view is anything you see beyond the room. For example, one client's home is wide-open. I made sure that we could "view" art-work from almost anywhere we sat.

ᘓ Organize remaining pieces of furniture to create balance —both optically and physically.

ᘓ Allow for comfort and easy traffic flow, being sure that the room accommodates its desired function. I recommend 28 inches as a minimum walk space, although I have used as little as 20 inches.

Meditations on a Big Change for Small Cost

PROVERBS 31:10, 13, 16-18

"A wife of noble character who can find? . . . She selects wool and flax and works with eager hands. . . . She considers a field and buys it; out of her earnings she plants a vineyard. She sets about her work vigorously; . . . she sees that her trading is profitable."

Day 1
Lord, teach me how to use time and money wisely, like the woman described in Proverbs 31.

Day 2
How can I work with the things I already have to make a better home?

Day 3
Teach me the proper balance between eager work and rest in Your restoring presence.

Day 4
You are a God who can do great works with ordinary people and small things. I praise You.

Day 5
What are Your purposes for me?

Day 6
Help me to seek Your will and approval first.

A Big Change for Small Cost

At some point, all people wonder what they have been created to do with their lives. What talents and abilities has God blessed you with? I thought about these things as I questioned my profession as an interior designer. I've been trained to make homes beautiful using the latest fashion trends and styles, and if that's not promoting a keeping-up-with-the-Joneses attitude, what is? But God was gracious to me. He showed me verse after verse about how, as a designer, I help families build homes with an atmosphere of joy and blessing. Even small changes can brighten up lives.

FRESH EYES

Many people have the misconception that interior designers will come into your home and impose their own ideas and styles on the family—and expect you to spend tons of money on things you probably don't need. In fact, good designers know how to stretch the dollar further and how to reuse what you have better than you ever imagined. They have a pair of fresh eyes to see the big picture and discover things that you forgot you owned. I often tell my clients that those who have the tightest budgets need a designer the most because they can least afford costly mistakes.

JUDY'S COLLECTION

One of my clients moved into a big old home. Judy loved to entertain and couldn't wait to throw a party. Unfortunately, the living room was completely empty. Buying furniture was out of the question because it was out of the budget! She challenged me to solve her dilemma.

Starting in the attic, I wandered through the house, gathering a little here and a little there. Before we knew it, we had three twin-sized mattresses with frames, five assorted tables, four assorted chairs, a grandfather clock, and a couple of small Oriental rugs. Judy got excited as we began to place these odds and ends in the living room. She gathered pillows, throws, a few plants, and some artwork. When we finished, the look was a wonderful eclectic blend of art and family history.

By combining art they had purchased along with the children's hand-painted creations, we amassed an art collection that was the perfect complement to the unique design scheme we had created for the space. To finish the room, we simply recovered the pillows and added some candles and a few other accessories to the fireplace mantel. It's been several years since I helped Judy, but other than adding to her art collection she hasn't changed a thing.

If you're ready for a change, here are some simple ways to make the most of what you have:

⊙ Start by emptying your room.

⊙ Take a tour of your attic, basement, and other rooms in your house. Try to *see* what is really there.

⊙ One by one, begin placing things into the space—starting with the largest pieces first.

- Strive for balance by using items that have similar scale. For example, don't combine a large sofa with a tiny chair.

- Use three main colors for your scheme to keep it cohesive.

- Have a reason behind putting pieces together. This is key to creating a successful eclectic style. If things don't look like they belong together, they probably don't.

- Test your new arrangement by taking a photo of the space or room. You will be amazed at what the camera reveals that you didn't see.

Meditations on Light and Shadow

REVELATION 21:23-24

"The city does not need the sun or the moon to shine on it, for the glory of God gives it light, and the Lamb is its lamp. The nations will walk by its light, and the kings of the earth will bring their splendor into it."

Day 1
God, Your light is so bright I can't look upon it, but I can enjoy its resulting warmth, illumination, and joy.

Day 2
Remind me that when I live in Your presence, You spread the light of Your love to every corner of my being.

Day 3
Am I hiding from Your light?

Day 4
How can I walk in Your light today?

Day 5
May my life bring splendor and glory to You.

Day 6
Fill my home with Your glory.

See photo #12

Light and Shadow

Lighting is probably the single most important aspect of our lives. It affects our mood, our ability to see and perceive beauty, and the appearance of colors. Interior design is complicated by the fact that lighting is both artificial and natural. The amount of natural light your home has is controlled by the number of windows and their sun exposure. Unless we start knocking out walls and adding windows and skylights, we cannot change our home's natural lighting. We can, however, do a lot to increase and control artificial light.

Start by examining your basic floor plan. It is essential to know what and where virtually everything will be placed into a space before planning lighting or electrical needs.

THINK IN THREES

There are three basic types of lighting—*ambient*, *accent*, and *task*. Ambient lighting allows the greatest diffusion, or spreading out, of light. Its job is to fill the entire space with soft illumination. Accent lighting highlights special areas or objects. The goal of task lighting is to provide the best possible light without a shadow or glare for a specific activity, like reading, for example. It is important to consider what kinds of lighting are needed for your spaces.

Light fixtures are designed to meet these three specific needs by design. Ambient fixtures can be ceiling-mounted styles that provide soft, general room light. Some popular choices are recessed cans or fluorescent fixtures that direct light upward. I suggest using a dimmer for ambient lights since you can change the mood and atmosphere by adjusting the level of light in a room.

Accent fixtures are usually chandeliers, pendants, track lighting, or recessed lights that are part of the ceiling. A very decorative lamp can also double as a piece of art. Accent lights can also be used to add extra light or focus to specific areas for such things as highlighting artwork or providing more light for dining.

Task fixtures can be similar to the other two in style or more specific. Besides your favorite reading lamp, recessed downlights and pendants that are installed into the ceiling directly over workstations can be effective task lights for the activity at hand.

PICK THE RIGHT BULB

It's also important to choose the correct lamp (or bulb) for each situation. Halogen lamps provide a clear, white light. Incandescent lamps generate a warm yellow or red light that we find soothing and flattering. Fluorescent lamps had a bad reputation of being a harsh light, but that is no longer applicable. In fact, fluorescent lamps have a wide range of colors (shades) designed specifically to accommodate many uses. Bluish white is the one we are all most familiar with, but lamps are available in warmer yellows, pinks, and even full-spectrum. Fluorescent lamps use one-third less energy than incandescent lamps and last twenty times longer.

Here are some tips for illuminating your home and life:

- To avoid casting your own shadow, install task lights slightly in front and above the surface where you will be working.

- When building a home and planning your electrical needs, err on the side of too many receptacles (or outlets) rather than too few. A too-dark space can be a continual source of frustration that may be expensive to fix.

- As you enter from the dark, the first light of the foyer should be subtle to allow the eyes an opportunity to adjust. Then as you progress farther into the house, the light can increase in volume and intensity.

- Always make sure that each space has additional lighting for such tasks as cleaning.

- Color-correct lamps are important for dressing areas. It's the best way to avoid the one-black-sock-and-one-brown-sock syndrome.

- A recessed light with a dimmer, placed directly above a workstation, can be an effective task light at 100 percent capacity, while acting as ambient light at 50 percent capacity.

Meditations on Getting Organized

1 CORINTHIANS 14:33, 40

"For God is not a God of disorder but of peace.... But everything should be done in a fitting and orderly way."

Day 1
Praise to You, God, for being a God who loves order and peace. Please bring order to my world.

Day 2
Forgive me for allowing disorder and conflict to reign in my home.

Day 3
Some days, Lord, I feel overwhelmed with confusion. Today, help me to take one thing at a time.

Day 4
Show me what is fitting and orderly in every situation. What can I do to bring more order to my life and home?

Day 5
When I am tempted to go to the opposite extreme from confusion and to make order an idol, help me to remember that godly order brings peace. Is my form of order bringing peace or strife?

Day 6
Help me to rest in the peace that comes from basking in Your love.

Getting Organized

We all love peace. A relaxing, safe, and well-organized home is the goal of every home-maker. Our homes, after all, should be reflective of what we are striving for in our daily walk as Christians. Our homes should bring smiles to our faces.

Unfortunately, if your life is like that of most people, you feel overwhelmed at the sight of your house—weeds in the front flowerbeds, stacks of unread mail and unpaid bills, seashells from your beach vacation two summers ago, not to mention piles of rotting laundry, the dust bunny colonies in full reproductive mode, and kitchen floors that rival the stickiness of iced cinnamon buns. For working women, the chaos of your professional life collides with the clutter of your home life. And for the stay-at-home mom, too often 5:00 P.M. arrives and babes in toy land are still in the living room, kitchen, and everywhere else!

CONQUER CLUTTER

How do you achieve a pleasing atmosphere at home? Organization is the key. Designing a system that meets the daily and weekly needs of your household, including the new treasures coming in and the old stuff going out, is not enough. You must have a method that works for you. Even if you have ambition and the help of hubby to tackle the project, your zeal can birth a system so complicated that only an engineer with a perpetual clipboard can maintain it.

Instead, pick two of your best friends—those who know your good and bad habits—and enlist them in helping you get a handle on the chaos and clutter. No one woman can be everything the Proverbs 31 woman was, but with the help of two good friends, you can multiply your progress.

ACCEPT WHAT WORKS

The secret to finding a system that works the way you do is to accept your own style. That's why having the help of friends that know you well is a good idea. I'm a pile-maker because I need to see it or I forget about it. My basement stairway has become the place where I can temporarily put things until I have time to get to them. I mounted a bulletin board just inside the doorway to the stairs. I put hanging baskets on the wall above the stairs where I place the "to be filed" mail and articles that I collect throughout the week.

When I have a few extra minutes, like when I'm on hold on the phone, I file them in large metal filing cabinets in my basement office. Once a year I ask my goddaughter to help me purge the filing cabinets and the piles that have accumulated around them. We re-organize whatever needs attention, tossing out-of-date material. My goddaughter has been helping me with this process every year during Thanksgiving break since she was ten. She's now sixteen and knows my system better than I do!

Here are some practical tips for keeping almost any space well organized:

- Label everything. It's the only way to be sure you can find it when you need it.

- Put your most frequently used items at waist height. Put the things least used higher up. Place things that are sometimes used on low shelves or drawers below waist height.

- Keep a step stool or ladder close by, so you can quickly reach things when you need them.

- If you have deep shelves, place the items in the back at a higher level so you can see them at a glance.

- Evaluate everything by the three-category process: Will I use it again? Is it worth storing? Should I throw it out or give it away?

- When designing storage space, be sure to plan for new items, or you will soon find yourself in the same disorganized state.

- Use clear plastic containers. They keep things neat, clean, and visible.

- Avoid the domino effect. Use shelf dividers to keep stacks in place.

- Take five minutes at the end of every day to clean out clutter, straighten up, and plan your to-do list for tomorrow.

Meditations on Master Bedrooms

HEBREWS 13:4

"Marriage should be honored by all, and the marriage bed kept pure, for God will judge the adulterer and all the sexually immoral."

Day 1
Forgive me for forgetting that You are a righteous and just God as well as a loving and merciful God.

Day 2
I don't like to think about sin, especially my own. Convict me, Lord, where I need convicting.

Day 3
Do I treat my sin casually?

Day 4
Help me to keep my marriage and my life pure.

Day 5
What can I do to better honor my husband?

Day 6
How can I make my bedroom a haven of love?

See photo #9

Master Bedrooms

When I was single, my bedroom, especially my bed, became a personal nest. I nearly "lived" in this space. I would gather everything I needed—my books, my cats, my favorite music and movies—and retreat! It felt wonderful. It didn't matter whether the sun was shining, the rain pouring, or the winter winds blowing. I felt comforted, cozy, and safe. It was my haven.

After I married Dave, things changed a bit. First of all, he doesn't like to watch movies in bed. Too bad! He's missing a good time to snuggle. He also likes to go to bed earlier than I do, which means it's nearly impossible for me to "nest" in bed. Oh well, sometimes we have to trade one wonderful experience for another. He's a keeper.

The master bedroom is the most personal space in the home. As a result it should truly reflect the personality of the couple residing there. It should be a couple's comfort zone. The key is to first determine exactly what your personalities and needs are and design around them. Too often our bedrooms become the catchall space. Before we know it, the entire world has invaded what should be a private and personal space.

DEFINE YOUR PURPOSE

If you suffer from insomnia, then I am sure you have heard the advice to use your bedroom only for sleeping. That way when you enter this room, your mind knows it has only one purpose in mind—sleep.

The reality of life can make this a difficult assignment to keep. Besides, many of us prefer to use our bedroom for multiple tasks and enjoyments. Most of us no longer have the luxury of using any room in our home for only one purpose. Our bedrooms have also become our home offices, exercise gyms, and dens. So we need to find creative ways of using space to accommodate our lifestyles.

By defining the space within a room, we can manage the clutter and regain control. Are there any tasks that could more easily be accommodated elsewhere in your home? Sometimes it is just a matter of changing your mind-set. Are you guilty of taking business to bed with you? Many of us are. In our time-crunched world, we are always behind in keeping up with our reading and can be tempted to take those memos, faxes, or reports into bed—just to do a little catching up. Before we know it, our bed has become an extension of our office. This is one place where I think we all need to say, "No!" Do that work someplace else. Your bed should be a sacred place . . . so keep those business colleagues out!

SOLITUDE CAN REFRESH US

Solitude is an underestimated necessity. Too many of us no longer find time to spend even a few minutes a day in solitude. Without it, we lose touch with ourselves. We no longer can identify those things that define who we are. Your bedroom can become a personal or couple's retreat. It can be the place where you can go off by yourselves to think, dream, write, or just sit and daydream.

Here are some ideas to help make your bedroom a retreat:

- The bed is the most important element in the bedroom. There's nothing like a restful night's sleep. If your mattress is more than ten years old, it's time for a new one.

- If you need total darkness to sleep well, then invest in room-darkening shades.

- Make a list of all the possible functions you expect your bedroom to meet. Think in terms of probability. You may dream of a reading corner, but in reality, you may never find the time to actually sit down and read.

- If exercise is one of your priorities and has to be done in the bedroom, define a specific area within the room to be conducive to exercise. If you make the process easy and accessible, you will stay committed to your goals.

- Be realistic about your expectations and recognize that your decisions are not cast in stone. Your bedroom's uses can continue to change as your needs change.

Meditations on Wallcoverings

PSALM 20:5

"We will shout for joy when you are victorious and will lift up our banners in the name of our God. May the LORD grant all your requests."

Day 1
In the days of the old covenant, each Jewish tribe carried an identifying banner. These banners were also carried into battle. If I were to design such a banner for my household, what would be on it?

Day 2
David, who wrote this verse, pledged loyalty to God by raising a banner to Him. How can I do that today?

Day 3
Banners were also used to celebrate and remember. What can I celebrate about my relationship to God?

Day 4
What victories has God given me?

Day 5
What room in my home could use wallpaper as a modern banner of celebration for life?

Day 6
May the Lord grant all my requests and those of my loved ones.

See photo #3

Wallcoverings

had the pleasure of working as the spokesperson for the Wallpaper Council for three years. I loved this job because it allowed me to talk about one of my favorite and most effective decorating tools—wallpaper. I fell in love with wallpaper as a child, so learning to use and hang it was natural for me. When I was thirteen, Mom allowed me to redecorate my bedroom. I hung an orchid, pink, gold, and white floral stripe wallpaper with just a little help from Mom. It's amazing the difference wallpaper can make in a space.

Wallpaper is art for walls. Did you know that artists hand paint the original pattern? It's a wonderful experience to see. I love the creativity in a wallpaper art studio.

INJECT A SENSE OF COZINESS OR SPACIOUSNESS

Wallpaper can make small rooms look larger, and large rooms, cozier. In general, light colors add a feeling of spaciousness. In particular, striped wallcoverings are a sure bet for adding height to a room. Stripes visually raise the height of the ceiling by drawing the eye upward. At the same time, pastel colors broaden a room and make the expanse of the wall seem larger. Together, subtle stripes and pastel colors can make a room seem bigger overall by drawing the eye both upward and outward.

Small prints help define a space and create a cozy, inviting atmosphere, such as in the kitchen. Mini-florals, fruits, and nature elements are "busy" designs that keep the eye focused within the room. Such patterns make the space feel more intimate. Borders can also work in conjunction with the small patterns.

Some patterns and colors can actually make us feel better. The key is to recognize your personality traits and complement them with the right color and pattern. If you feel stressed at the end of the day, then decorate your resting spaces, that is, your reading room, bedroom, or den, in paler colors that will help you calm down. If you suffer from lack of sunlight, use sunny yellow to perk up your spirit.

USE A SIGNATURE PRINT

Choose a print you love. This will be your "signature print" or "banner" that will set the color scheme for the room. Signature prints usually contain several colors in a large-scale pattern. Let one color from your signature print dominate. Use this color in as much as two-thirds of the available area. Pull two to three other colors from your signature print to act as support or accent colors. Use them in smaller areas and in accessories. Carry your color scheme throughout the entire house to create strong visual continuity. Varying the dominant color and patterns you use in each room, while remaining faithful to your basic color scheme, will keep your home interesting, yet unified.

Wallpaper may even improve your children's IQs. If you want to encourage your baby's ability to recognize objects, large-scale patterned wallpaper is the best choice. Choose a variety of nice shapes, remembering that a baby can only see a up to eight to fifteen inches. Use a large-scale pattern near the crib, such as one of the wonderful large vertical borders. Another option is to use a horizontal border. If you place it near the crib, the baby will have something to look at when awake, giving Mommy a little breathing time. Primary colors, especially red, are best for young children. Pastels are best used for "sleeping" areas. By combining both primary and secondary colors, a scheme can last through your child's kindergarten years.

Choosing color and pattern doesn't have to be scary if you take the time to evaluate your space. Think first about practical aspects of the room such as these:

- Function: How is the room used? Warm colors work well for active rooms; cool colors for relaxation areas.

- People: Who will use the room? Consider their color preferences when selecting your color scheme.

- Location: What is the exposure to sunlight? Northern and eastern exposures benefit from warm color schemes; western and southern exposures, from cool schemes.

- Size: Do you want to increase or decrease the apparent size? Warm colors advance, making the room seem smaller; cool colors recede, making the room appear larger.

- If you have never hung wallpaper, don't start with the kitchen or bathroom. Although those rooms may have the smallest wall space, they tend to require the most cutting.

- Hanging wallpaper with your spouse is *not* a good idea, no matter how much you love each other. Do your marriage a favor, and ask a friend to help you. Better yet, hire a professional if you can afford it.

Meditations on Bringing the Outdoors In

PSALM 52:8-9

"I am like an olive tree flourishing in the house of God; I trust in God's unfailing love for ever and ever. I will praise you forever for what you have done; in your name I will hope, for your name is good. I will praise you in the presence of your saints."

Day 1
Even the house of God has green growing things in it!

Day 2
The thought of spring and trees flourishing revives me. I'm energized to get up and get moving.

Day 3
Praise the Lord for springtime!

Day 4
Praise the Lord for the promise of new growth!

Day 5
Praise the Lord, for You are good. Let my mouth praise You to those around me, especially my family and neighbors.

Day 6
May my family and I flourish as olive trees rooted in Your unfailing love.

See photo #8

Bringing the Outdoors In

A s I sit at my desk looking out the window, I am thrilled to finally see green! After a cold, snowy Pennsylvania winter, green is a great sight. Medical professionals say that by looking at green grass for ten minutes we can lower our blood pressure. Imagine how much benefit you can get from incorporating a little outdoors everywhere in your home. Okay, maybe you don't want to order a dozen olive trees from the garden catalog, but even a touch of greenery will do.

LIGHTEN UP!

Summer decorating has a light touch: light colors, lightweight fabrics, and even lighter-colored furniture. It's the optical weight that matters. The lighter the colors, the lighter the room will feel.

Start the lightening process with your windows. If you have heavy draperies, think about exchanging them for simple sheers for the summer. If that isn't practical, try this idea. One of my clients has rich gold-and-cream-striped silk brocade drapery panels at either side of her large window. For the summer we simply attached a sheer panel of gold fabric to the inside of the existing side panels. Using a tassel tieback, we pulled the sheer fabric back, creating a soft swag—which instantly lightened the feel of the window.

If you're decorating color scheme is dark, try adding more of the lightest shade with accessories such as pillows, artwork, or tabletop items. Or add a light neutral such as cream or yellow as your summer accent.

With the popularity and availability of slipcovers, a summer makeover is simple for your furniture. Transforming the dark green velvet sofa to a garden oasis of fabric flowers is good for heart and soul!

ACCESSORIES TO THE RESCUE

I like to change accessories with the seasons. This is one of the simplest ways to incorporate the outdoors into your decorating. I start with my dining room table. I remove the winter brocade table runner and the leather books, as well as the winter dried floral arrangement. In their place I use a white, cut-lace table runner, wicker birdcage, and spring flowers. Since the beach is my favorite place, I always use shells for my finishing touch. This simple change immediately lifts my spirits!

What better way to bring the outdoors in than with fresh flowers? Add baskets or vases of flowers to tabletops, countertops, or even shelves. Branches of forsythia or dogwood can be a decorative treat for the eyes. Use silk flowers wherever fresh flowers are impractical. I recently made silk nosegays to hang from my doorknobs. Now every time I open or close a door, I am delighted with this special touch. The same idea can work for the back of a chair or the center of your bed's headboard.

SOMETHING FOR EVERY STYLE

For a formal theme, use sophisticated botanical prints and add floral arrangements of summer blossoms in crystal vases. Topiaries are not only the perfect formal complement, but they are also quite stylish.

Garden-style furniture pieces blur the line between indoors and out. Rearranging or exchanging some of your heavy winter furniture is another way to bring the outdoors in. Replace occasional furniture with wicker or rattan. Place a whimsical garden ornament among a group of terra-cotta pots filled with your favorite summer plants.

Don't forget the little nooks and crannies of your home. A simple garden bench placed at the indoor entrance to your home can bring an immediate bond to the outdoors. Fill your kitchen window with an indoor herb garden or pots of wheat grass. My cats love this idea!

If you have a remodeling project planned, consider some of these ideas for keeping the spirit of outdoors in your decorating year-round:

- Use bamboo flooring. It's beautiful and natural!

- Install a garden window. Check out the new renaissance, conservatory-style wood garden windows with gothic, arched styling (www.sunroomco.com/garden-windows.htm).

- Add floor and wall coverings of wicker, bamboo, sisal, and grass cloth.

- Furniture made with coco bark and abaca mixed with wood, leather, and glass creates an informal interior.

- Add a tropical flair with lamps and fans, from faux bamboo chandeliers to palm-covered, ginger-jar shaped table lamps.

Meditations on the Challenge of Little Blessings

PROVERBS 22:6

*"Train a child in the way he should go, and
when he is old he will not turn from it."*

Day 1
What a huge responsibility parents have. At times I get overwhelmed.
I feel so inadequate.

Day 2
Thank You, Lord, for small signs from You and from my children that I am
training them in the way they should go.

Day 3
Thank You for a sloppy kiss at bedtime, a bouquet of dandelions present-
ed as if they were roses, an urgent petition for someone other than themselves, a temptation resisted, or a wise decision made away from home.

Day 4
Father, protect the children I love from physical and spiritual hazards.

Day 5
Grant me patience, gentleness, wisdom, and diligence as I guide these
little ones until they go off on their own.

Day 6
Where do I need to improve in training my children or guiding someone
else's child?

The Challenge of Little Blessings

From the moment your children were born, you wrapped your arms around them and swore you would care for them and protect them always. Yet, from the minute they were born, your job became preparing them to be self-sufficient and leave the nest. As one mom put it, "Someday, God willing, my grown daughter will stand as tall as I do. And when that happens, the tiny person I love so passionately will live only in photographs, home videos, and my mind." The challenge is getting these precious gifts from infancy to adulthood in one piece and with at least some of our hair intact. It's amazing how different children within one family can be.

When my sister Wendy was little, she was a climber. Without fail, she would end up in the hospital emergency room at least once a month. My mother says it is a miracle that she was never arrested for child abuse—no child could get into that much trouble! One night when she was three, Wendy got up long after bedtime, climbed up on the bathroom sink, opened the medicine cabinet, and managed to down an entire bottle of baby aspirin. Then she quietly returned to bed, waking several hours later with a tummy ache. Thank God for tummy aches and hospital stomach pumps.

CURIOSITY IS NATURAL

If you have a child like Wendy, creating a safe home is tough. These precocious investigators love to test boundaries. The more barriers you place for their protection, the better they get at scaling them. If there's a dangerous spot in the house, they will find it. Their natural curiosity causes them to taste, touch, and feel the world around them. It is how they learn, which makes it all the more difficult because you don't want to quell natural instincts for learning while you are training them about ways they shouldn't go.

ACCEPT YOUR LIFE STAGE

Many of my interior design clients need encouragement to recognize and accept their particular phase or stage of life. This is especially true for first-time moms. Life before baby was about building a pretty nest. Life after baby is about creating a safe nest. As long as there are babies and toddlers in the home, sophisticated decoration cannot be the top priority. Decorative candles and other accessories will disappear, and "fashionable" baby gates and child-proof doorknobs will multiply. The fireplace mantel will be wrapped in protective cushioning, and ribbons on toilet paper may greet guests. Life won't always be this way, but it's best to arrange your home for the comfort of your family. Doing so will mean less stress for you.

Here are some things that you may have overlooked when childproofing:

> Keep dangerous items in your garage stashed safely away inside a wire mesh pen. Your children may know those things are off-limits, but it takes only minutes for a neighbor child to harm herself.

- Store garage door openers out of reach.

- Test your automated garage door by placing a cardboard box in the way of the door as it closes. If it crushes the box, it can crush a child.

- Be sure all storage cabinets are securely locked.

- Plastic bags can cause suffocation. In the kitchen, be sure they are tucked out of reach.

- Take extra caution with a wet floor. A slippery spot can send a toddler flying.

- Never let children of any age eat or suck on anything, such as hard candy, while lying down.

- Place an infant or child's bed away from the window. Also check window coverings for potentially hazardous pulls or too-long cords.

- Secure throw rugs with a rubber mat. My brother broke his leg on a loose throw rug.

- To prevent an excited child from running into a sliding glass door, mark the window with decals or decorative tape placed at child's eye level.

- Pad the bathtub waterspout. Flexible rubber hosing works great.

- Check the railings of your staircase balcony to be sure they are close enough to prevent a small child from slipping through. Three-foot-high mesh can easily be installed to the inside of the railings for protection.

- Pray *aloud* for a hedge of protection for your precious cargo every morning and evening.

Meditations on Family-Friendly Designs

PSALM 127:3

*"Sons are a heritage from the LORD,
children a reward from him."*

Day 1
Thank You, Lord, for blessing me with children—whether they are biological, adopted, step-, god-, or surrogate.

Day 2
Help me to remember that I do not own my children; they are a heritage from You.

Day 3
Forgive me for sometimes viewing children—my neighbor's or mine—as burdens and annoyances.

Day 4
Remind me that all children are a precious reward from You.

Day 5
How can I treat my children as gifts from God?

Day 6
How can I teach them about their heavenly Father?

Family-Friendly Designs

Can you imagine what it would feel like if, upon arriving at your new heavenly home, God cautioned you to be careful not to get the rug dirty as you entered? What if God asked you not to sit on the heavenly sofa but to sit on the floor? Unfortunately, for some children this is exactly what it's like in their homes.

LOVE THE ONES YOU ARE WITH

My mother's best friend, Terry, never married and never had children. My mom has six children. Terry's home life was and always will be quiet, neat, and perfectly under control. Obviously, as our family grew, Terry's ability to cope as a guest in our home became more and more strained until she finally took a tranquilizer before coming to visit. Not that our home was chaos, it's just that six children of varying ages and genders made for a loud and lively home, something Terry wasn't used to. For her, it was like walking into a cyclone!

Families come in all shapes and sizes. The addition of one more child can even push the limits of a seasoned mother. Whether it's your own new baby or a visiting neighbor or family member's child, it's amazing how much one more child can change the normal routine and peace within a home. I don't have any children, and yet, if I had a choice, I would much rather be in a home with children running about. Their youthful spirit makes a home rich.

PLAN FOR CHILDREN'S NEEDS

Children have specific needs within a home. It takes effort and patience to create a home that is comfortable for children and adults alike. The important thing is designing family-friendly rooms. As one designer put it, "Love seats and two-seater sofas are too small for family life. Cuddling with a puppy, a spouse, and a four-year-old attached to several armloads of toys demands a long, deep sofa."

Children can be taught to be respectful of certain possessions within their environment, but that list should be short. Your home should not require that you wrap your children in plastic and follow behind them with paper towels. They need spaces where they can play and enjoy themselves without worrying about the furniture. Don't make the mistake some mothers make of trying to keep a spotless house and making the children feel that they are less important than those things.

Here are some family-friendly decorating tips:

- No matter what you think about the beauty of tile, stone, or other hard floor coverings, they were not designed for children. Even a wood floor needs a little carpeting to soften the blow when that little chin hits the floor.

- Square corners on tabletops are an accident waiting to happen. Choose furniture with rounded corners.

- Pretty accessory items sitting on top of anything within a child's reach should be removed.

- A big trunk or other decorative box for the family room is the perfect place to put all the day's favorite toys.

- Choose dirt-colored fabrics. That way when they get dirty, no one will notice.

- Choose washable fabrics and slipcovers for all your upholstery items.

- Consider having your chair-seat fabrics laminated with a non-shiny vinyl coating. It's a breeze to wipe clean.

- Tape electrical cords out of harm's way with duct tape.

Meditations on a Safe Haven

1 SAMUEL 25:35

"Then David accepted from [Abigail's] hand what she had brought him and said, 'Go home in peace. I have heard your words and granted your request.'"

Day 1
Abigail was wealthy, yet her home was not immune to outside threats of violence. Help me to remember that my times are in Your hands, Lord.

Day 2
Abigail delivered food to an angry man and averted a crisis—an invasion of her household by David and four hundred of his warriors. Are there conflicts looming in and around my home?

Day 3
Quicken my heart as You did Abigail's so that I am aware of possible threats and can neutralize them with kindness as she did.

Day 4
Who feels unsafe in and around my home? Bring potential problem areas to my attention, Lord.

Day 5
Abigail took steps to ensure peace and safety in her home. How can I do that in my home?

Day 6
Grant my loved ones and me Your protection over my home.

A Safe Haven

I recently read an article in our community newsletter titled "Welcome Burglars!" It got my attention. Obviously, no one would intentionally post such a sign, but the article pointed out that many of us inadvertently invite trouble. It takes three things for criminal activity to occur: someone with criminal intent, a place for it to happen, and an opportunity. We can control only one thing—opportunity.

The article said that effective crime prevention could mean simply closing your garage doors. Burglars often pick a nice neighborhood and drive around looking for the welcome of an open garage door. But there is more we can do.

BE PROACTIVE PSYCHOLOGICALLY

There are physical and psychological aspects for providing a safe haven. Children, with their innate wisdom and sensitivity, detect an adult's fears and will internalize these fears. From a psychological perspective, my friend Louise Dietzel, M.A., suggests specific things parents can do to help: "Parents must take charge of their own feelings. The younger and more dependent the child, the greater chance of the child absorbing the adult's fear." Louise says that keeping kids safe begins in the hearts of parents. Parents have two choices, love or fear. Love teaches and invites love; fear teaches and invites fear. Each parent's choice has far-reaching effects for the parent and the child for the rest of their lives.

David wasn't a criminal, but he felt that Abigail's husband was treating him unfairly. That's why he and his warriors were on the prowl. Creating a safe environment means taking a proactive as well as a defensive posture. Abigail initiated kindness to David, and we can do the same with our neighbors. Getting to know them is one way we can psychologically promote a safe-home zone.

MAKE PHYSICAL CHANGES

I know from experience working with and interviewing children that simple physical changes can make a difference. For example, when young children are frightened in the middle of the night, they run to their parents' beds. When older children get frightened, they run to their own beds. When I ask children of all ages to name the most important element in their bedroom, they all say the bed. It is their safe haven. It's no surprise that so many young girls want a canopy bed since the cocoon effect makes them feel safe. By involving your children in the choices within their bedrooms, they not only take ownership and care of their rooms but also have a place where they can feel confident and safe.

Having a place that feels safe is especially important for children who come home to an empty house every day, especially for those who will be alone until dusk or later. Making sure your children are and feel safe is critical to their physical and emotional well-being.

Here are some simple tips for making your home a safe haven:

∞ Cover exposed windows. Windows without covering leave children feeling vulnerable and exposed after dark. They see only the black of night staring at them. A simple shade changes all of that. It gives children a sense of control and security within their environment.

∞ Provide and review security measures with your children. Be sure they know what to do if someone attempts to break in while they are home alone.

∞ Consider creating a "safe room" within your home with an interior dead-bolt lock. Be sure to include a cell phone, which is fully charged with a speed dial code for 911.

∞ Install fire extinguishers strategically throughout your home. Teach your children how to use them properly.

∞ Be sure your children know a neighbor they can contact should they not be able to reach you in an emergency.

∞ Start a neighborhood-watch program and report suspicious activity.

Meditations on Peaceful Boundaries

PROVERBS 15:25

*"The LORD tears down the proud man's house
but he keeps the widow's boundaries intact."*

Day 1
I don't like to think of the Lord tearing down anyone's house. Help me to remember, O Lord, that You are a God of justice.

Day 2
How can I keep my house from becoming a proud woman's house?

Day 3
I praise You, Lord, that You protect the widow and what rightfully belongs to her.

Day 4
Lord, I feel safe when I remember You are looking out for widows and for me and my best interests.

Day 5
Are there boundary issues that I am fretting over or arguing about?

Day 6
How can I trust the Lord to keep my boundaries intact?

Peaceful Boundaries

Now more than ever, it is important to be at peace with our neighbors and to feel a sense of community. Through community we can watch over and help protect each other. The key to creating a bond of community is to know and respect those we live near. Sometimes that can be difficult.

Several years ago, Deb and Ken were involved in an ongoing dispute with their next-door neighbor over their adjoining property line. The problem with this "fight" was that the neighbors refused to talk. They showed their contempt with their actions.

Deb and Ken did all they could to figure out and resolve the crux of the problem, which seemed to be a crooked fence that was mistaken by the neighbors for a boundary line. Finding the boundary pins only made matters worse. So Deb and Ken mentally "loaned" three feet along the side of their yard to their neighbors.

They trusted that God would eventually take care of the problem. He did. Soon those neighbors moved. Ken and Deb raised the boundary markers and tied red flags to them. They greeted their new neighbors warmly, told them about their crooked fence, and lived happily ever after.

PARTY POOPER OR PROTECTOR

The value of a home is so important that it's easy to get defensive. Sometimes the defensive action is motivated by good intentions for the protection of others.

For example, my backyard has the best hill for sledding in the community. Not having children of our own, my husband and I loved to watch delighted kids as they raced down our hill on every imaginable kind of sled.

While conversing with my insurance agent, I innocently mentioned the thrill of the sledding hill. The look on his face was my first clue that I could be in trouble if a child got hurt in our yard. We live in such a litigious society that innocent fun can turn into serious trouble. My husband and I had to establish some boundaries.

Now, if children want to play on our hill, we warn them that their parents must be present and take all responsibility for their safekeeping. I feel like the big, bad fun wrecker of the neighborhood. Nonetheless, it has become a lesson for adults and children alike regarding respect for boundaries in the neighborhood.

MUTUAL RESPECT

Being a good neighbor involves more than just holding block parties and having fun. It is about understanding the individual personalities and needs of your neighbors and respecting them. Sometimes a neighbor has a reputation for being crabby. If we discover what lies behind that—i.e., he has an elderly parent, ill spouse, or wayward son or daughter—we can be more understanding about certain demeanors. Such knowledge gives us an opportunity to be a good neighbor. Other times, we must patiently pray for the "neighborhood nasty" and trust God to do the rest.

National Good Neighbor Day is the fourth Sunday

in September. Here are some ideas for celebrating it all year long:

- Respect the privacy of others to make them *happy* neighbors.

- Take responsibility for your pets.

- Keep quiet. Don't mow your lawn, trim your shrubs, blow your leaves, or use your snowblower at the crack of dawn or the stroke of midnight, and follow your local noise ordinances.

- Greet your neighbors, regardless of how long you have lived near them. It's never too late to make a new friend.

- Start a neighborhood newsletter.

- Prepare meals for the elderly and shut-ins.

- When you borrow something, return it quickly and in better condition than when you got it. Or fill it with a present, like cupcakes in a borrowed muffin tin or flowers from your garden in a borrowed bucket.

- Before beginning any new building project, whether it's a storage barn or a goldfish pond, check to be sure it is within your boundary lines.

- Alert your neighbors to any construction you are planning. Ask their permission if it requires their side yard to be an egress during construction.

- Be sure your outdoor lighting is neighbor-friendly and does not glare directly into your neighbor's bedroom windows.

Meditations on Caring for Heirlooms and Treasures

2 TIMOTHY 1:14

"Guard the good deposit that was entrusted to you–
guard it with the help of the Holy Spirit who lives in us."

Day 1
With what have I been entrusted?

Day 2
Salvation, Scripture, and heroes of the faith are precious to me.

Day 3
Thank You, Lord, for all my blessings.

Day 4
Help me to take good care of the legacy of love from my family, as well
as the material possessions I have received from others.

Day 5
I need You, God, to enable me to guard what You have given me. Thank
You for the help of the Holy Spirit.

Day 6
How can I better display and care for my family heirlooms?

See photo #10

Caring for Heirlooms and Treasures

D eb has a child's rolltop desk at the entrance to her living room. The end of one leg is broken, the hardware is loose, and the caned seat is missing. Sometimes the "little desk" is a bother, but no one thinks of putting it in the attic or basement.

When her husband was a boy, he used this desk that had belonged to his father. The Strubel family will states that this desk is to be passed down to the oldest son. Since Ken's older brother does not have children, the desk was given to Ken and Deb's son, the oldest male Strubel grandchild. Until she can get the seat recaned, Deb covers it with a small quilted wall hanging from her grandmother. Deb feels privileged to keep a family treasure as a way to honor her husband's family and give her son a sense of his heritage.

APPRAISE THIS!

Deb's family isn't the only one to discover the blessing of family heirlooms. Decorating with antiques has garnered a broad audience because of the popularity of such TV shows as *Antiques Roadshow, At the Auctions,* and *Appraise It.* So why are we suddenly so interested in collecting and decorating with antiques? Author Caroline Clifton-Mogg says, "We are defined by the past, not the present. . . . Furniture or objects from another place or country . . . have a romance and a history not shared by our other acquired possessions."[1]

Family heirlooms keep alive the history of loved ones now gone. I think our personal treasures, and the stories behind them, add pleasure and character to a home. A home is far more than architecture. It is an assimilation of our history and our life experiences.

HOMES KEEP FAMILY HISTORY ALIVE

Precious stories, history, and memories can fill our hearts with satisfaction. Just the idea of being able to tell and retell the story of Pop Pop's little desk while actually sharing it with the next generation provides a sense of family connectedness and honor. It is an intensely personal, almost spiritual blessing, which can only be experienced by the physical passing down of such an item. Allowing children not only to see, but also to touch, use, and make the heirloom a part of their lives teaches a tender appreciation for things old.

Here are some tips for caring for your antique treasures:

- Accept that the patina of collected dirt and discoloration is part of the treasured asset of the finish.

- When dusting antiques, use a clean, soft cotton rag. Do not use spray or liquid cleaners.

- For carved-wood details or gilded areas, use a large sable artist's brush for dusting.

- Glassware should stand upright, not touching another. Wash in moderately hot water and mild detergent. Avoid wiping gold or other metal-banded pieces while the glass is hot.

To remove white rings on wood tabletops, rub the spot with a mixture of mayonnaise and toothpaste. Wipe and then polish.

For all you headhunters: always vacuum your stuffed moose head from the snout up. Use the furniture attachment of your vacuum and go with the grain of his coat. (This tip is from Kovel's Quick Tips.)

NOTE

1. Caroline Clifton-Mogg, *Decorating with Antiques* (New York: Bulfinch Press, 1999).

Meditations on Space for Temporary Residents

2 KINGS 4:9–10

"She said to her husband, 'I know that this man who often comes our way is a holy man of God. Let's make a small room on the roof and put in it a bed and a table, a chair and a lamp for him. Then he can stay there whenever he comes to us.'"

Day 1
Thank You, Lord, for blessing me with a home that I can use to minister to others.

Day 2
Help me use my wealth, however small and insignificant I may feel it is, to provide comfort for those around me.

Day 3
Who in my world needs a place to call his or her own?

Day 4
Lord, show me what space I can set aside and maintain for a special person—a stepchild, college son or daughter, in-laws, or other visitors.

Day 5
Grant me creativity and insight as I choose furnishings and accessories for others.

Day 6
May the people who stay in the spaces that I create enjoy them and the fellowship in my home.

Space for Temporary Residents

Have you ever felt homeless? I have. Sometimes when my travel schedule gets hectic, I feel like a nomad or a refugee, carrying my belongings on my back or dragging my suitcase behind me. One time just as I finished unpacking, I discovered some unwelcome little critters in my room. The hotel was brand-new, and management was quite embarrassed. They kindly moved me to a new room, which meant that I had to repack, move, and unpack a second time. I was exhausted.

That experience got me thinking about others whose circumstances require them to move from place to place—stepchildren, college students, speakers, and those in ministry. For them, *home* is often a stepparent's house, someone's den, or a hotel room.

Making your home a place that welcomes these transients requires special attention. You want to nurture both their physical and emotional well-being—even if only temporarily.

STEPCHILDREN NEED A SPACE

Children's rooms are just as personal and important to them as the master bedroom is to you. Stepchildren, who sometimes live with one parent and then the other, need special consideration. They need a place to call their own—even if it's just the corner of a bedroom. If possible, be sure they have their own bed. Something as simple as a bookcase that is only for her use can be enough to give a stepchild a sense of ownership.

My goddaughter, whose parents are divorced, often sleeps over at my house. We have made sure that she always has a room in our home to call her own. When we were in the process of moving and building a new home, she was concerned about her belongings. We packed her things in boxes that were clearly marked as hers. It was important to her to know where those boxes were at all times. It gave her a sense of belonging, security, and control.

When we finally moved into the new home, she wanted her new room to be just as it was in the old house. For her, this is the one constant that she can count on. Today, if someone else comes to visit, I honor my goddaughter by asking her permission to use the room—even though she always says yes.

CONSIDER A COLLEGE CHILD'S COMFORT

College-aged children can feel displaced or devalued when parents are too anxious to turn their old rooms into dens or offices. If you eliminate their rooms, they feel as though they have no place to call home. Always think twice about changing the room of a child away at school—even if he or she says it's okay. While they want to appear strong, often they are not emotionally ready for that kind of a change in your home.

The transient person in your life may not need a large space, but he or she does need some privacy and a sense of belonging. Here are tips for making children welcome in your home:

- Allow children to be involved in the decorating process of their rooms. The more involved children are in decorating, the greater their sense of ownership. Children who have a sense of ownership take better care of their rooms.

- Monogram towels for all the children in your home—stepchildren included.

- Don't remodel children's rooms without discussing it with them first—no matter how old they are.

- Allow visiting children a place to keep cherished items safe—a special chest, a pretty box, or a bureau.

- Use built-ins to add extra space to a shared bedroom.

- Take advantage of any wall space by building wall-to-wall, ceiling-to-ceiling bookcase storage units.

Meditations on Designing a Homework Center

2 TIMOTHY 2:15 NKJV

"Be diligent to present yourself approved to God, a worker who does not need to be ashamed, rightly dividing the word of truth."

Day 1
How am I training my children to be diligent in all they do, including homework?

Day 2
Forgive me, Lord, when life gets too hectic and I get impatient.

Day 3
What am I doing for my children that they should be doing for themselves?

Day 4
Am I diligent to present myself approved to God? Do I study the Word?

Day 5
How can I set an example of diligence at home and work?

Day 6
Does every family member have a comfortable place in which to study? Lord, show me what I can do to make hard work more attractive to others.

Designing a Homework Center

In many families, just saying the word *homework* can raise blood pressure, send some children running, and put others into total despair. It is important to note that the attitudes and habits that start when people are young usually follow them through college. For parents, this can be extremely frustrating. If you homeschool, there is an even greater need to set aside specific areas for learning and study.

There have been several studies in both homes and classrooms about what kind of environments best promote study and learning. Using this information to design a homework center for your children may make the homework process easier for you and them.

Designing a child's work space is different than designing a work space for an adult. As always, function must come first. For example, you may need to provide a durable surface that can be cleaned easily after the use of markers, pencils, and paints.

CHOOSE HAPPY COLORS

One of our strongest emotional responses is to color, so color is critical to a child's ability to be happy and functional. I have found that people have the strongest emotional responses to blue and green. We usually love one and dislike the other. Be sure you know what your child likes since a "green child" can be miserable or even agitated when placed in a blue environment. I use fabric swatches to learn quickly a child's preference for color and pattern. I believe by providing a colorful scheme you will promote energy and inspiration.

Just this week while working with a three-year-old, I was reminded of children's amazing color sense. Hannah couldn't wait for me to come with my color box to choose the paint color for her room. When I asked her what color she wanted, her immediate response was "Green!" I showed her a color deck of greens. Without hesitation she began going through it until she found the perfect shade of bright mint. I could not have chosen a better color for Hannah. Her creativity is evident and strong. Mint green is perfect for her. Children have an innate sense of what colors make them happy, and a happy child is a productive child.

THINK ABOUT LIGHT AND COMFORT

Safety, comfort, lighting, and acoustics should be considered when designing a homework center. Light—especially natural light—is vital to our physical and emotional well-being. A quiet space is more conducive to study. Be sure to anchor files and other heavy items to the wall to prevent them from falling over and injuring someone. Children always test the limits of furniture, so make sure that your furniture choices are strong and stable. Built-ins are the easiest way to get the most room out of any space. Use the vertical space only for items children don't need. Otherwise, they will climb to reach them!

Parents need the ability to easily monitor the homework area. Here are some quick tips to consider:

- Try using the dead space at the end of a hallway. It may make the perfect place for a homework center.

- Children love to sit on the floor (actually, I still prefer to sit on the floor!), so having carpet on the floor is critical to making it comfy.

- Be sure the desk includes a large work surface and comfortable chair that encourages good posture.

- Purchase an adjustable keyboard for the computer, which ensures safe keyboarding without creating repetitive-stress injury.

- Encourage children to make the space their own by framing and hanging their artwork.

- Use stackable cubes, shelving, and even a wall of shelving where books and other resources can be stored.

- Place an "in" and an "out" box for homework.

- For shared spaces, provide individual cubes or storage areas. Set specific time schedules if children share the computer. Boys can monopolize the computer, leaving girls little time to work on their computer skills and homework.

- Be sure each child has her own homework kit with such items as pencils, erasers, markers, crayons, a stapler, tape, a glue stick, and a ruler.

- A pile of large stuffed animals or a beanbag chair under a window or floor lamp can become the perfect reading nook. Hang a few plants; they are good for the spirit and the body.

- Encourage children to take a few minutes each day to review tomorrow's schedule and pull together the items they will need. Have them use this time to clean and reorganize their work space. This is a good habit that promotes productivity, organization, and picking up after oneself.

Bathroom Sanctuaries

The bathroom can provide a quiet sanctuary that allows you to refresh the body and spirit with a place for meditation and relaxation.

See page 137

①

Firm Foundations

My family's strongest bonds were built in the kitchen—preparing meals,
doing laundry, eating, and laughing—this is where our foundations were built.

2

See page 13

Wallcoverings

3

The large-scale floral pattern
of this wallpaper adds depth
and color while providing a
cohesive element for creating a
romantic decorating scheme
that perfectly unites furniture
and space.

See page 61

Viewing Your Blessings

Encourage your heart and inspire your work by creatively arranging, in a balanced composition, family photos and mementos into your workspace.

④

See page 205

Living in the Great Room

See page 37

This furniture arrangement allows everyone to enjoy the fireplace and the television. It is well organized yet inviting with comfortable seating.

⑤

Accessories

A vase of large pink tulips in full bloom are the perfect starting point for this composition.
Following the rule of tallest to smallest—creates a balance of accessories perfect for this tabletop.

6

Fabulous Focal Points

Your eye is immediately drawn to the fireplace—which is architecturally focal in this room. The entertainment center balances the weight of the window on the opposite wall, creating an optically proportioned space that functions beautifully.

See page 41

7

Bring the Outdoors In

8

This room feels like an extension of the garden with its light colors, lightweight fabrics, and garden style furniture. An open window with just a touch of sheer fabric allows the outdoors to flow in, creating a sunfilled space for winter or summer.

See page 65

Master Bedrooms

This master bedroom is as beautiful as it is organized. The seating area for reading is enhanced with natural light from the window. The bed is central and focal when you enter the room. A cheerful wall color with pretty red accents makes this the perfect couple's retreat.

Caring for Heirlooms and Treasures

Family treasured antiques give this room a sense of history and romance. The wallpaper border and chandelier complement the Victorian furnishings for a room that invites you back into another time and place.

See page 85

Seating

Be sure to have a variety
of seating choices so
everyone can find a place
to sit comfortably.

See page 105

Light and
Shadow

This kitchen basks in light and shadow because its
lighting plan includes ambient light from the chandelier above the table; under cabinet accent lighting; and
task lighting provided by the recessed ceiling fixtures.

See page 49

Letting Your Candlelight Shine

The simplicity of white tapered candles placed in a variety of holders and sconces around the room creates a special ambience that can only be achieved with candlelight.

See page 129

13

Meditations on Expanding Outdoors

MATTHEW 12:34-35

"Out of the overflow of the heart the mouth speaks. The good man brings good things out of the good stored up in him, and the evil man brings evil things out of the evil stored up in him."

Day 1
Probe me, Lord. What overflows from my heart?

Day 2
Forgive me for impatient thoughts and harsh words.

Day 3
Set a guard over my mouth, Lord.

Day 4
Renew my heart, so that it is filled with the knowledge of Your goodness and love.

Day 5
Please make my love for You and others increase and overflow so that I may be a source of joy.

Day 6
How can I overflow with good things today?

Expanding Outdoors

Is your home feeling cramped? If so, why not expand your living space to the outdoors? No matter the size of your yard, you can always find a few spare square feet that can be transformed into an outdoor sanctuary. Each spring, I take the walking garden tour in our community. I love the amazing outdoor living spaces that are carved into the tiniest of city yards. The creative use of space, materials, and plantings never ceases to amaze me.

Having grown up in the inner city, I have fond memories of the front porch—from noisy sleepovers to afternoons practicing my accordion (blessings on my poor neighbors)! Our porch was the center of summer living and community interaction. It's no wonder that today's most popular new communities include front porches.

Backyard patios, porches, gazebos, and gardens have created new decorating delights and challenges for all. From trellises and pergolas to awnings and waterfalls, our lives are overflowing into creative new spaces. Homeowners are going to great lengths to create living areas that serve as extensions to their homes, including complete outdoor kitchens for Italian-influenced Alfresco dining—and not just in year-round warm climates! Today's outdoor kitchen appliances are as sophisticated as those used indoors. One dear older gentleman even had cable TV hooked up on his little porch, so he could enjoy watching summer sports outdoors.

PLAN FOR LOW MAINTENANCE

As I struggle through the last months of winter each year, I begin planning my outdoor decorating projects for the spring. It just isn't spring for me until I have my porch cleaned and dressed for outdoor living. My porch, complete with a nostalgic, old-fashioned glider hanging from it, is a refuge and a gathering place. Very little maintenance is needed since the floor decking is a splinter-free wood/resin combination that doesn't require any sanding or oiling. Because the railings are PVC, they require no painting. And it's screened-in, so we enjoy the outdoors without worrying about the bugs and weather.

DON'T FORGET TO DECORATE THE GARDEN

If a garden is your idea of outdoor living, then consider decorating it too! Latticework, trellises, arbors, and benches are just the beginning. Your garden, like your home, should reflect your personal decorating style, whether formal or fanciful. One memorable garden included colorful old shoes balanced on random wood stakes. As the blooming season came to an end, the maze of shoe flowers took over the show! Another included an old iron bed filled with flowers—now that's a true flowerbed! Don't forget to carve out a little living space in your garden. A couple of Adirondack chairs under an old elm tree or a Victorian metal bench beside a garden wall can provide the perfect afternoon respite.

A few years ago, I had the pleasure of researching sleeping porches for HGTV. Did you know they date back to Greco-Roman times? Of course, we can't forget the stories of the Arabian nights and their luxurious pillows and fabrics. There is a theory that the reason southern porch ceilings were painted blue was to mimic the color of the sky; others say it cools things down. I think sleeping porches will be the next out-door living boom. Imagine nestling in a lace-trimmed hanging bed on a screened porch with candles glowing in the evening dusk. I can hear the cicadas and feel the evening breeze. Can't you?

Here are some things to consider as you plan your outdoor rooms:

- If your idea of "outdoor living" is climate controlled and dirt-free, then consider a four-season room with operable windows!

- Sticking to an all-white decorating scheme allows nature's changing palette to dominate.

- For upholstered furniture, choose the new weatherproof fabrics. They look and feel like regular fabric, but they are designed to handle the outdoors.

- For an open porch, make and hang curtain panels from window screening edged with an outdoor fabric to keep unwanted critters out. Add outdoor fabric panels for privacy.

- Invest in outdoor lamps. They are weighted at the bottom to keep them stable during inclement weather. Be sure to use shatterproof lightbulbs also. They are covered with a thin plastic film that keeps the glass from shattering if they break.

- Coordinate your color scheme by painting your plastic, PVC, or metal furniture with the new paints designed specifically for these materials.

- Consider permanent or retractable awnings to add a little shade where needed. Some styles have removable screening.

Meditations on Cleanliness

PSALM 51:1, 10

"Have mercy on me, O God, according to your unfailing love; according to your great compassion blot out my transgressions. ... Create in me a pure heart, O God, and renew a steadfast spirit within me."

Day 1
Have mercy on me, O God, even though I'm undeserving of Your great compassion.

Day 2
Wash away my sins and make me whiter than snow.

Day 3
Give me a desire to do Your will.

Day 4
Fill me with joy and gladness as You teach me wisdom.

Day 5
Let me not remember the transgressions of others, and help me show compassion to all in my household—even the messy ones.

Day 6
What praises can fill my mouth today?

Cleanliness

Growing up in a household with six children was a great study in contrasting levels of cleanliness. My three sisters shared a bedroom as teenagers. Two of them were typical of most teens—their focus was not on tidiness. One sister, however, was and still is Miss Clean. Her side of the room, which was marked off with masking tape, glistened with perfection. As you can imagine, she did not peacefully coexist with her two siblings.

The good news is that most teens' rooms are not reflective of the kind of housekeepers they will become. Statistics show that as teens become adults they gain a healthy respect for the things they have paid for and purchased themselves!

TO EACH HER OWN

Even so, early in their adulthood, the three sisters still did not agree on how clean a home should be. Two of the sisters married young and had the good fortune to be stay-at-home moms in the first years of their children's lives. Even with three young children, you could literally eat off Charlene's floors *every* day of the week! Dian was more relaxed. Her baby was her primary focus, not her house.

One day while she was visiting Dian, Charlene asked, "How can you stand having dirty windows?"

"Do they bother you?" Dian responded. "Then *you* clean them!"

On a practical level, this is a good concept. In most families, you will find several levels of cleanliness within the home. Ultimately, the person who cares the most should clean that area! I know that clutter makes me crazy. My husband, on the other hand, loves to make it. He must be comforted by it because he surrounds himself with lots of it. I can only handle so much clutter, and then I get frantic. At one point I was so desperate to get him to clear out his clutter that I tried to convince him we had to move. It didn't work.

Now, I do my best to avoid going into my husband's clutter domain—the way parents learn to shut their teen's bedroom door. When my husband's stacks begin invading the rest of the house, I take action and move them nearer to his upstairs chaos.

AGE MAKES A DIFFERENCE

For most of us, our stage of life dictates how clean our homes will be. According to the iVillage Web survey on housekeeping habits, the 5,717 women who responded proved that there really is a generation gap. Women over the age of fifty-five do the most cleaning—nineteen hours a week versus close to fifteen hours by younger women. Most women over sixty say the messiest room in their homes is their bedroom, but women between the ages of thirty-one and fifty say their children's bedrooms win that prize. Also, 51 percent of women over sixty never go to bed with dirty dishes in the sink, but 47 percent of younger women say they do that all the time.

As an interior designer, I see just about every level of cleanliness—and perceived cleanliness. Yesterday, I visited a semiretired client. As we approached the dining room, she began apologizing for the mess.

"This is one of the cleanest homes I have ever been in," I said, laughing. "I wish my home was as clean this!" I have two cats, as did this client. Yet even on the cleanest day of the week you will find not one, but two, cardboard scratching pads in the middle of my living room. Yes, this is where they belong. It is how I keep my cats from scratching furniture.

If you have small children, allow them to play freely in at least one space. Spend your extra time playing, laughing, or just listening to your children. The old adage "give it a lick and a promise" is good advice. The years of childhood pass quickly. Enjoy them. You can clean house when they leave home.

In the meantime, to make the cleaning process easier try these ideas:

- Listen to books on tape or your favorite music while cleaning. As a teen I always listened to music when cleaning. Why did I ever stop?

- To teach good habits to kids, set aside regular cleaning times each week for the whole family to straighten up the house. It's a great way to reduce overall clutter and finally locate the missing homework assignment.

- When dusting, use paintbrushes (my favorite is a round, long-bristled craft brush) to dust cracks and hard to reach places on electronics, etc.

- To remove permanent marker from counters, use hair spray. It works like magic.

- To clean screens, use a nylon-covered sponge.

- Use hydrogen peroxide to remove blood from furniture or clothing.

Meditations on Seating

REVELATION 3:21

"To him who overcomes, I will give the right to sit with me on my throne, just as I overcame and sat down with my Father."

Day 1
What does it mean, symbolically, to be seated with Christ in heaven?

Day 2
Help me to live my life on earth remembering that by Jesus' sacrifice for my sins I will live forever in heaven.

Day 3
Thank You, Jesus, that I don't have to depend on my own strength and ingenuity to get a seat in heaven.

Day 4
Thank You for forgiving me and giving me the power to overcome.

Day 5
I praise You, Jesus. You were faithful to the Father's will.

Day 6
Help me to trust You to overcome the trials of life.

See photo #11

Seating

D o you remember the story of Goldilocks? She found three chairs in the bears' home. After trying and rejecting two, she declared of the third, "This one fits just right!"

Many years ago I had a friend named Bob who was 6'5" tall. He loved coming to visit my home. Why? He felt comfortable because I had furniture that fit him. What makes this interesting is that I am only 5'1". My furniture was comfortable for both of us because it was an overstuffed, plop-yourself-down sectional. By arranging the pillows and the ottomans, it could accommodate a person of any size.

Bob often complained about how uncomfortable he was at his son and daughter-in-law's home. It's no wonder, because they had small-scale, delicate, antique Victorian-style furniture throughout their home. I'm not sure Bob ever told them he was uncomfortable, but I know he would have visited them more often if they had owned at least one chair in which he was not afraid to sit. He told me he was always afraid of breaking and ruining a family heirloom.

IF CHAIRS COULD TALK

Being given the right to sit with God at His throne would be an honor above all. We show honor to guests at a meal by where we seat them. Men are often given the seat at the head of the table to show respect for them as heads of their households. Children know it's a big deal to graduate from the children's table in the kitchen to the adults' table in the dining room. It only makes sense to choose chairs to fit those sitting in them.

Child-sized furniture has been around for centuries. There is something so adorable about furniture made just for children. Children feel important if they have a seat of their own. From a child-sized eighteenth-century Chippendale chair to a floral-clad overstuffed upholstered chair, there's a style to fit every room.

THE TALE OF THE TALL CHAIR

My parents had a chair that all of us children called the "Queen's chair." It was a large white leather chair with a tall back, like a wing chair but with high wooden legs. Sitting in that chair could be good or bad. If we sat there by choice, it made us feel like royalty, sitting high above the other children. Other times, Mom and Dad would instruct us to sit in that chair. Then we were in deep trouble and about to get the lecture of our lives for bad behavior! If it were not for God's grace, we would all be in a similar position as we anxiously await our turn before the throne of the Almighty.

While you wait to take your heavenly seat, here are some tips for picking good earthly chairs:

- Never attempt to purchase a chair for someone other than yourself unless you have the same body dimensions and proportions.

- Pay attention to seat depth. Choose a seat that allows you to sit all the way back for support and still reach the floor with your feet. Otherwise, you will strain your knees or your back.

🕭 When choosing upholstered chairs, both the seat and the back cushion construction are important. Be sure to ask about each. A chair with an attached tight back will be firmer than a loose cushion back. Most good manufacturers allow you to change the construction of the seat cushion to suit your preference, from soft, cushy down to firm foam.

🕭 If you have back trouble, choose a firm seat. I like a firm cushion with a soft top.

🕭 The heavier the person, the more support that is needed.

🕭 Choose a good fabric based on its content and construction to meet your specific durability needs. Poor quality fabric will show wear quickly.

🕭 Read and follow the fabric cleaning instructions.

🕭 On wooden chairs, look for a support bar between the legs.

🕭 If the salesperson says the chair has a lifetime guarantee, ask whose lifetime it refers to—yours, the chair's, or his?

Meditations on Easy Entertaining

HEBREWS 13:2

"Do not forget to entertain strangers, for by so doing some people have entertained angels without knowing it."

Day 1
How am I forgetting to entertain strangers?

Day 2
Even my neighbors are like strangers. How can I
get to know them better?

Day 3
Lord, who else do You want me to show hospitality to?

Day 4
Remind me that entertaining is a way of loving others
as brothers and sisters.

Day 5
How can I make all my guests feel as comfortable and loved as family?

Day 6
God of peace, calm my racing mind and squelch my search for
perfection the next time I entertain so that I can focus on my guests.

Easy Entertaining

My mother's home has always been filled with people, laughter, fun, and food—the more the merrier. Friends, neighbors, and perfect strangers are welcome. Even today, with all of us grown up, Mom's house is where we go for every holiday, birthday, or other event worthy of a gathering.

The secret to my mother's success in creating this wonderful atmosphere for celebration is her realistic expectations. She accepts the size of her home, its condition, and her budget for entertaining. Of course, it doesn't hurt that she's a fabulous cook and loves people. She never puts on pretenses. She does not try to impress with airs of grandeur, and she is comfortable with herself. That makes everyone else comfortable.

DECORATING AND THE ART OF ENTERTAINING

There are similarities between decorating and entertaining. In fact, an upcoming celebration is often what prompts people to redecorate. The success of decorating and entertaining is dependent on a key realization. Your lifestyle and your personality should be the determining factors for how you decorate and also for the kind of entertaining you do. That's something my mom truly understands.

When decorating for a family gathering, consider and accept the reality of your home and family. No matter how you try, you can't turn couch slouches into fancy formals just by purchasing formal furni-

ture. You'll only set yourself up for disappointment.
The same is true of entertaining. If you're really a
chili person, don't try to serve a seven-course
gourmet meal. Serve chili out of a bucket! Let everyone come in jeans and be comfortable. In other
words, if you're not Martha Stewart, don't pretend
you are.

PLANNING IS IMPORTANT

Just like with any decorating or renovating project, planning is the key to successful celebrations.
One of the biggest mistakes people make in decorating is running out and buying the first thing they find
just because their mate is finally agreeable to purchasing a new sofa, and they want to get it before the
company arrives. Unfortunately, although it may be
new, it probably wasn't what you wanted. After the
party is over and everyone goes home, you're stuck
with that oddball sofa!

The same is true for entertaining. Don't wait until
the last minute and hurriedly invite tons of guests
and purchase the first supplies you find just to get the
job done. By doing so you will likely end up with a
gathering that's not what you wanted, or you'll wear
yourself out, becoming too tired to enjoy the celebration yourself. Tired and cranky hostesses make for
miserable guests. After the guests leave and you are
left with the cleanup, you will be tempted to take out
your frustration on your immediate family or your
dog. Junior and Spot will both learn to hate parties.

Here are some successful celebration tips:

Make your guests the focus of the event.

Families love to reminisce. Bring out old photos and include them in your table decorations.

If you have a small home, do a buffet.

If you have a small dining room or none at all, set up small tables throughout the house—in the living room, dining room, or even the foyer.

When possible, have an outdoor party. A deck or patio party can be a real treat.

Use an unusual centerpiece. It doesn't have to be flowers! Try a bowl of polished stones (less than two dollars a pound at most pet or garden supply centers). Or make a cornucopia of dewy vegetables by polishing them with a spray of water and oil.

Write a detailed to-do and shopping list. Then begin two weeks ahead of time to get it done. If necessary, store items in a separate area to keep others from eating or undoing before the day of the party.

Plan an easy main course; for example, a one-dish meal like stew, paella, casserole, or curry paired with rice.

Find a reason for a celebration and enjoy!

Meditations on Fantastic Flooring

EXODUS 3:4–5

"God called to him from within the bush, 'Moses! Moses!'
And Moses said, 'Here I am.'
'Do not come any closer,' God said. 'Take off your sandals,
for the place where you are standing is holy ground.'"

Day 1
God, are You calling me? Am I listening?

Day 2
Help me always to respond to You as Moses did: "Here I am."

Day 3
How can I cherish my personal access to You? How can I remember I'm
on holy ground when I enter Your presence?

Day 4
What sins do I need to take off just as Moses took off his sandals?

Day 5
O Lord, forgive me for treating my floors and carpets as if they are holy.

Day 6
Teach me to remember that You are holy.

Fantastic Flooring

This week I am installing everything for a Parade of Homes house, which is part of our regional Building Industry Association's annual showcase contest. Of course, the weather is not cooperating, and it's been pouring rain all week!

The builder insists that we remove our shoes every time we enter the home. Imagine four deliverymen holding a thousand-pound marble dining table attempting to remove their shoes as they enter the doorway. Right! They are not magicians, and I do not own a magic wand. It's not as if the floors are spotless; they have not yet been cleaned of construction grime. As the furniture delivery truck drove up, I was sweeping the dining room floor.

ANALYZE YOUR TRAFFIC PATTERNS

I have a healthy respect for homes, but sometimes people get carried away. For most folks the reason is simple: they probably purchased the wrong kind of flooring for their lifestyle. With all the choices available today, there is no reason for that to happen. So, where do you begin? There are lots of things to consider when deciding what flooring to use.

Here come the questions:

- Do you use the front door, the back door, or the garage door?
- How do you get from the kitchen to the bedroom or family room?

⊘ Do you use the patio door to get to the deck in the summer?

⊘ Will messy food, like ribs smothered in barbecue sauce, be carried in this area? If so, be sure to choose an easy-to-clean surface. Carpet would not be my choice.

⊘ Do you take your shoes off the second you walk in the door?

⊘ Do your kids and husband also remove their shoes? Do they remember to wipe their feet?

⊘ Does your dog wear boots in bad weather? Probably not, so where do you clean his feet? (I use a bucket of warm water on the deck and dunk a paw at a time.)

CARPET OPTIONS

I have nearly white carpeting, but it is *not* near any of the entry points of my home. I used hardwood flooring or resilient (vinyl) flooring near all door-ways. Yet technology has made carpeting softer and more durable than ever. Most carpets carry a ten-year warranty and will clean up well as long as you follow the manufacturer's suggestions for maintenance and cleaning. Milliken Carpet has a revolutionary prod-uct: residential carpet tiles you can install yourself. When one carpet tile gets stained or damaged, you can easily replace that square. Now that's a smart idea!

Do you have young children that will want to skate, ride, race, or jump rope on your floors? Young children also tumble and fall, and a hard surface like ceramic tile can be very painful. Today's laminate floors are nearly indestructible and much easier on falling bodies.

I could go on forever about different possibilities that you could consider, but the point is for you to think about your needs, not a magazine's showcase floor or your neighbor's plush palace. Obviously price, appearance, and your heart's desires have a lot to do with your final selection. Sometimes it's best to choose something temporary until circumstances change. Choose products for their properties as well as their appearance and price. In other words, choose products that will promote a happy home life!

Here are some questions for special consideration:

- Do you have any family members in a wheelchair or using a walker or cane? Stay away from area rugs.

- Do you have kitchen chairs with wheels? (They can really fly on a tile floor!)

- Do you sew or have other hobbies or crafts? Is there the possibility of losing things like pins, tiny nails, or other microscopic items in deep pile? If so, you may want to consider resilient flooring or commercial carpeting.

- How old are your pets? The older they get, the less control they have. If you have indoor cats, at some point they will throw up inside. Use something easy to clean.

- Do you live near the beach? If so, sand is an issue. Stick with area rugs over durable flooring.

- Is the soil in your area rich and red? That's great for growing, but horrible for carpeting.

Meditations on the Wonder of Pets

LUKE 12:6

*"Are not five sparrows sold for two pennies?
Yet not one of them is forgotten by God."*

Day 1
You are an amazing God! I praise You!

Day 2
Thank You for being the kind of God who cares about animals—
even the common sparrow.

Day 3
Thank You for not forgetting about animals and pets.

Day 4
How can I be a good caretaker of Your creation?

Day 5
What or who am I forgetting to care for in the world around me?

Day 6
What can I do to better share in Your delight of animals?

The Wonder of Pets

More than half of all US households have a pet. According to the National Institutes of Health, there are 56 million cats, 51 million dogs, 45 million birds, 75 million small mammals and reptiles, and uncounted millions of aquarium fish. What makes these facts so amazing is that God knows and cares for each one. And sometimes He gets a little help from us.

BENEFITS ABOUND

What is it about pets that makes us willing to put forth so much time, effort, and money to keep them? They are clearly part of God's plan. The reliable and unconditional companionship offered by pets can be very rewarding and beneficial to our physical and emotional well-being. Studies have shown that having a pet can help lower heart rates and blood pressure, relieve stress, and actually add years to our lives.

Companion pets can positively influence child development. Studies reveal that children who have pets have better social skills, more empathy for others, and more self-esteem. Children can also learn responsibility, gentle handling, animal behavior, and the facts of life and death with a pet.

Even some of the old theories about children and pets are being proven wrong. Most studies now show that children that were exposed to at least two cats as infants have fewer allergies, not more.

JUST PART OF THE FAMILY

Growing up, our family always included a variety of pets. You name it, and we probably had it. Even today, all of us, including my mom, have pets in our homes. My husband and I have what some might consider an odd combination. We have two cats: seventeen-pound Percy and a delicate longhaired one named Miss Peony. We also have a bird haven in our backyard with five feeders, several birdhouses, a birdbath, and a hummingbird feeder. In the eight years that we have lived there, we have had only one fatality. Miss Peony learned her lesson early and now is a bird-*watcher* rather than a bird catcher.

OUTSIDE CREATURES TOO

Once the birds outside learn to depend on you for food and water, it's important to keep providing it for them. It's a lot of work, but the rewards are worth it. I love listening to them sing as they flutter about the yard.

This spring we had the unexpected pleasure and trial of having a nest of five baby birds in our front door wreath. We managed by creating a blockade with burlap and stakes to keep the cats off the front porch. A homemade sign attached to the burlap notified visitors and deliverymen to please use the back door to keep the little ones safely in their nest. I must say, I do question mother bird's choice of location for her nest. Now that they have flown the coop, I wonder whether to replace the wreath or do without.

If you have or are considering a pet for your family, here are some things to think about:

- Just like with children, you must pet-proof your home. Lock cabinet doors to keep little paws from opening them. Keep trash cans covered or safely behind locked cabinet doors. Never leave out ribbon or plastic Easter basket grass because it can be very harmful to your pets if they eat it.

- Bundle dangling wires from VCRs, TVs, stereos, and telephones.

- Move houseplants out of reach. Be careful not to accidentally close your pet in a closet or clothes dryer.

- Be sure your garage is safe by keeping rakes and shovels out of the way, so they don't get knocked over. Clean the floor of any oil or antifreeze puddles since one lick can be deadly.

- Keep foods out of reach. My first dog, Ginger, managed to eat two pounds of cookies in one sitting. She was a very sick puppy for several days.

- Consider an invisible fence. It works great for dogs and cats alike. We have one, and it was the best investment we could have made for our cats.

- Two cats of the same gender work best. It eliminates the who's-in-charge syndrome once they have reached adulthood.

- Treat all animals with respect. Never make a dog growl, bark, lunge, or otherwise act aggressively.

Meditations on a Pleasing Aroma

LEVITICUS 2:1–2

"When someone brings a grain offering to the LORD, his offering is to be of fine flour. He is to pour oil on it, put incense on it and take it to Aaron's sons the priests. The priest shall take a handful of the fine flour and oil, together with all the incense, and burn this as a memorial portion on the altar, an offering made by fire, an aroma pleasing to the LORD."

Day 1
There's something comforting about knowing that God has
a sense of smell, that He loves pleasing aromas.

Day 2
As I launder sweaty socks and clean out smelly refrigerator growths,
may the labor of my hands be pleasing to God.

Day 3
Lord, help me to view all my home and family duties as offerings of love to You.

Day 4
May my thoughts, words, and deeds be like grain, oil, and incense
that combine as a memorial portion on Your altar.

Day 5
Thank You for the biblical truth that our prayers rise to You in heaven
like fragrant incense.

Day 6
Do my words and actions smell like a pleasing aroma to the Lord?
If not, what changes do I need to make?

A Pleasing Aroma

Are indoor odors worse in summer or winter? In my opinion, it doesn't matter. In the winter we keep our homes sealed tight to keep the warm air in. In the summer we keep our homes sealed tight to keep the warm air out! The bottom line is we've created an environment that is perfect for creating a stinky home. Whether it's cooking odors, pet odors, or just plain smelly socks—it's all unpleasant. Some odors, however, are worse than others.

THE NOSE KNOWS

I hate walking into my house at the end of the day and smelling the morning cat food! Trust me. Stale shrimp is bad! Of course, that is not the only ugly smell caused by our loving pets. When we first moved into our home, our male cat decided to mark his territory by urinating. Although we have repeatedly had those few spots professionally cleaned, every now and then I get a leftover whiff. The right temperature and humidity level create the perfect climate to remind us of the area that belongs to Percival Van Mouser.

GRACE SCRUBS US CLEAN

The lesson here is relevant to our spiritual lives. The Father's grace scrubs us clean, but every now and then, we give in to human weakness and smell like old sins again. Fortunately for us, our Father's cleansing comes with a lifetime warranty. All we have to do is make the call.

If only it were that easy to rid our homes of unwanted scents. Foul odors can invade even the tidiest of homes. All too often we may not even be aware that our homes smell badly. The next time you return home, take the time to slowly walk through your home and pay close attention to how it smells.

Bacteria are the prime source of most household odors. A foul-smelling garbage disposal or ripe garbage pail can make even the loveliest of homes uninviting. Dampness caused by poor ventilation can produce odor-causing bacteria. Fortunately, there are some common household products that can eliminate most unpleasant odors. Baking soda, vinegar, lemon juice, rubbing alcohol, and cat litter can do more to freshen the air than a battery of caustic cleaning products. The fundamental way to prevent odors is to eliminate the source.

Here are some helpful hints for making your home smell as fresh as spring air:

- Use ice cubes made of vinegar and water to safely clean and freshen your garbage disposal. Grind the vinegar cubes in the disposal. The vinegar acts as a cleaning agent while the ice sharpens the blades.

- Place a pan of white vinegar on the stove and let it simmer to get rid of strong cooking odors.

- Ventilation is an effective means of keeping a house smelling fresh. In addition to opening a window now and then, open closet doors and dresser drawers regularly. Never place damp clothing into a closet or dresser drawer.

- Periodically launder your pet's bedding. If your pet has a favorite spot on the floor or in a chair, place a towel or other washable item there.

- Locate the source of urine smells by using an ultraviolet light (available at pet supply stores). Urine stains luminesce under ultraviolet or black light.

- Freshen a musty trunk by pouring cat litter into a large, uncovered coffee can. Place the can in the trunk and close the trunk lid. In most cases the odor will be gone overnight.

- To freshen home accessories (pillows, blankets, children's toys), sprinkle baking soda on them, and then wipe off.

- Odors from pet urine are hard to eliminate, but these steps can help. Treat the spot with a product containing liquid enzymes. Soak the area with the enzyme. It may take several treatments. Don't use ammonia-based cleaners; they can compound the problem.

- My husband collects antique children's books, which often have a musty smell. To get rid of this odor, we store them in a paper bag filled with crumpled newspaper. Repeat this process several times using fresh newspaper each time until the odor is gone.

Meditations on Outbuildings

1 TIMOTHY 6:17–19

"Command those who are rich in this present world not to be arrogant nor to put their hope in wealth, which is so uncertain, but to put their hope in God, who richly provides us with everything for our enjoyment. Command them to do good, to be rich in good deeds, and to be generous and willing to share. In this way they will lay up treasure for themselves as a firm foundation for the coming age, so that they may take hold of the life that is truly life."

Day 1
Lord, You have given me so much by way of possessions.
Help me to share with others.

Day 2
May I value the forgiveness and "the life that is truly life" that comes through Jesus Christ more than anything else.

Day 3
In what way ought I be storing up treasure in heaven?

Day 4
Of the things and wealth that You have richly provided for our enjoyment, help me know what to give away and what to keep and where to store it.

Day 5
If I were to have additional space, how could I share it with others?
How can I bless others with the space I already have?

Day 6
Is there a space that I could make that would allow for spiritual retreats?

Outbuildings

When I was a child, my dad built a playhouse in the backyard. It was the size of most sheds, but it had cute shutters on the window and a screen door to allow a breeze without bugs! We loved our little house. We held sleepovers there. We put on plays from it, even charging the neighbors five cents to watch. While we loved it, I now realize that Mom and Dad must have, too, since our being there gave them some added peace and quiet.

CREATURE COMFORTS

Today as we look for ways to expand our living spaces in an outrageously expensive real-estate market, the old shed has become the most versatile outbuilding. The backyard shed can double as a home office, TV room, reading nook, or even a guest room. And backyard buildings aren't limited to utilitarian-drab. Everything from screened gazebos to fancy tree houses has become nearly standard backyard fare. Peter Nelson, author of *Home Tree Home,* explains that today's tree house usually comes with all the creature comforts, including electricity and plumbing—if allowed by zoning.

Zoning restrictions are the first thing to check if you are thinking about building your own home extension in the backyard. Every municipality and township has its own set of codes. Most don't allow for plumbing or overnight guests; nevertheless, some folks are using their outdoor rooms for overnight events.

Victorian-style backyard houses are extremely popular. You can purchase detailed plans or kits that are ready to assemble. They are the perfect family project. Most have enough headroom for adults and an adult-sized Dutch door, which makes them great for garden storage, pool houses, or any other storage need. Such an outbuilding can be passed down from one generation to another. *Early Childhood Link* is a great resource for many different styles of ready-to-assemble outdoor playhouses. Two people can assemble most in a day.

A FAN'S DELIGHT

I know one gentleman who built himself an outdoor room for watching football! It sits on the hill in his backyard. I laughed the first time I saw it, but his wife is thrilled. Now she can do or watch what she wants indoors while he cheers for the team in his hilltop shed. Summerhouses, those without insulation, are usually made from cedar or redwood, which are durable, easy to maintain, and resilient. Summerhouses are not just an American phenomenon; one Web site in the United Kingdom has a summerhouse collection of Georgian-style buildings that come complete with tongue-and-groove floors. They are supplied ready glazed, which means the windows are already in place, and are easy to assemble in sections.

FIRM FOUNDATIONS

These outbuildings can serve as additional rooms of the house for rest, reading, recreation, entertaining, or storage. A place to keep outdoor equipment and toys can keep your garage and closets cleaner and less cluttered.

Below are some things to consider when building your own outdoor space:

- Do you need a building permit or planning permit from the local zoning board? Is the building to be constructed over an easement? How will the building be used?

- If your garden shed has cedar siding, you have several finishing options you can consider:

  1. Let the cedar siding weather naturally. Cedar siding contains naturally occurring oils and organic compounds that allow the wood to resist sun, water, and insect damage.

  2. Use a wood sealer to block the pores of the wood.

  3. Apply an exterior stain or paint the cedar siding. This third option requires the most maintenance.

- Many of these outbuildings have no foundations. They simply rest on solid concrete blocks spaced at two-foot intervals. Crushed gravel can be used to level the blocks if your lot is relatively flat. If your lot is sloped, you may have to use posts, which project from the floor system to the concrete blocks. People who live in a cold climate should place the concrete blocks or posts on concrete piers.

- If you live in an area subjected to high winds or storms, include special anchors at each corner of the building. Without this protection, your building can be blown over or across your yard.

Meditations on Letting Your Candlelight Shine

LUKE 11:33

"No one lights a lamp and puts it in a place where it will be hidden, or under a bowl. Instead he puts it on its stand, so that those who come in may see the light."

Day 1
God, thank You for sending Your Son to earth to be our light.

Day 2
Thank You for eyes to see both physical and spiritual light.

Day 3
Thank You that the truth of Your Word can dispel spiritual darkness.

Day 4
How am I leading others toward the light of Christ?

Day 5
How have I hidden my lamp?

Day 6
What can I do so all who enter my home see the light of God's love?

See photo #13

Letting Your Candlelight Shine

The spiritual light in this verse is Christ. The physical light is a candle. Candles are the oldest means for supplying light. Although a number of changes have taken place in the process, the basic method for making candles has remained the same. Most candles are made by the timeless process of placing a cotton wick into wax, which is then molded, dripped, extruded, pressed, rolled, drawn, or filled into a desired shape and size.

Reference to lighting candles dates back to ancient times as early as the thirtieth century B.C. in Crete and Egypt. Candles are mentioned in biblical writings as early as the tenth century B.C. A fragment of a candle was found in Avignon, France, that dated from the first century A.D.

That's amazing, considering Deb has trouble keeping her candles more than a year. She once stored a box of them in her attic and was amazed a year later to discover that they had "miraculously" disappeared. All that remained were some limp wicks, strange little metal contraptions, and an oily bunch of clothes in the box underneath. Did I mention that Deb is blonde?

The quality of candlelight depends upon the type of material used. For a brighter light, beeswax is best. I guess the same thing could be said of our spiritual light. If we want Christ's light to shine through us, the basic recipe hasn't changed. We must know and use His Word as our wax of choice. A fragment of knowledge can only provide a dim light. But much knowledge of His Word can keep our spiritual candles burning bright. In the case of spiritual light, I guess it's okay if our wax "disappears" into the people around us the way Deb's candles melted in her attic.

MORE THAN DECORATION

People have enjoyed using candles for centuries. Their color and scent enhance everyday life and evoke memories. While no longer man's major source of light, candles continue to grow in popularity and use. Today, candles are used for decorating accents, celebrations, romance, and special ceremonies. They cast a steady glow for all to enjoy.

The Jewish Festival of Lights, or Hanukkah, began in 165 B.C. This eight-day celebration centers on lighting candles, feasting, and exchanging gifts. It is the historical celebration of the Jews' successful revolt against the King of Syria's mandate that his subjects worship the Greek gods.

CANDLES SAY "CELEBRATION"

Candles are intrinsically connected to many events in our lives, such as birthdays, holiday dinners, and religious celebrations. In ancient times, tradition decreed that a candle be lit at the time of death to prevent demons from stealing the soul of the dying. The Greeks and Romans lit candles to accompany the dead to their last home. Until the fifteenth century, church candles were made of beeswax because it was thought that bees originated in the Garden of Eden. The Puritans primed their Christmas candles with a bit of gunpowder to usher Christmas in with a little flash—and you thought Puritans were no fun!

Recently, candles have become a part of our everyday lives as well. They add warmth, style, and an inviting mood to any room. I hope that my spiritual candle does the same.

Here are some tips for safely using and decorating with candles:

- Combine candles of uniform color in a variety of shapes and widths. Don't be afraid to use a variety of candleholders as well. The trick is using one color to keep the elements unified.

- For an elegant look at dinner, try placing different height tapers in a straight line down the center of your dining table. Place them about three inches apart.

- Don't use scented candles for a dining table centerpiece. The combination of food and candle odors might be unpleasant.

- Never leave a burning candle unattended. If you have pets or children, keep lit candles out of reach and use a candle chimney to be safe.

- Prior to each use, trim wicks to one-eighth or one-fourth inch in length.

- Before lighting, be sure your candleholder is meant for use with a lit candle and not just for decorative purposes.

- Do not use a candle when one-half inch or less of wax is left.

- Avoid putting candles in drafts. It is not only dangerous to surrounding materials but also makes the candle burn faster.

- Fill a crystal bowl with water and add a few floating candles for a romantic centerpiece.

- My favorite idea is to place a column candle in a pottery bowl and surround it with seashells or pretty stones.

Meditations on Choosing and Using a Designer

"Plans fail for lack of counsel, but with many advisers they succeed. A man finds joy in giving an apt reply–and how good is a timely word!"

Day 1
How am I attempting to go at life alone?

Day 2
Why have I failed to ask for counsel?

Day 3
Lord, help me find wise advisers.

Day 4
Enable me to accept good advice.

Day 5
May I give joy to those who encourage me with a timely word.

Day 6
What timely word can I give today?

Choosing and Using a Designer

'll never understand why some people hire interior designers and then fail to take their advice. I'm not just saying this because I'm a designer. Deb feels the same way. Her husband is a painting and decorating contractor who has to apply the customer's final decision. More often than you would guess, his clients tweak their designers' choices in an attempt at perfection. The results are a disappointing mismatch.

WHO IS THE PROFESSIONAL?

Too often, I end up being the third wheel in a decorating project. A mother, aunt, or "well-meaning" friend decides that they know better than the client or me! Just yesterday I witnessed a sweet woman being manipulated into shopping for something other than what she wanted because her *friend* knew what was best. One of my clients, a bright and capable middle-aged woman, is still attempting to decorate her home by only choosing things her mother likes. It's so sad. It reminds me of the way we sometimes don't follow God's Word and listen to our peers instead.

WISE DESIGNERS LISTEN TO YOU

Other people don't or won't hire an interior designer because they are afraid that their home will end up reflecting the designer's tastes. This could not be further from the truth. Capable, qualified, sincere designers want to make you happy. Interior designers who are members of the American Society of Interior

Designers (ASID) have the training and expertise to manage all the details of your project. They know the importance of listening to your ideas and understanding your needs. From consultation to planning to the finishing touches, they can help you at every step and add value to your budget. All ASID members agree to abide by the Society's "Code of Ethics and Professional Conduct."

In my twenty-nine years of practice, there have been only a few times that a client and I decided not to work together. Those decisions were made because our personalities did not mesh. The main component to any good relationship—professional or personal— is compatibility.

COMMUNICATION WORKS BOTH WAYS

Communication, too, is a major factor in the success or failure of the client/designer relationship. Unless a client tells me that something is wrong or they are not happy, I cannot fix the problem or apologize for it. One couple, with which I thought I had good rapport, suddenly turned silent. I placed a follow-up call a few days after the installation. I left a voice message but never heard back from them. I continued calling and pleading on their voice recorder for them to please call me.

Finally, they did. They were afraid that nothing could be done with a cornice board that arrived that they thought was too deep. Therefore, they chose not to call. Instead, they were trying to accept something that didn't look good. I told them I was more upset at the fact that they felt they couldn't come to me than I was that they had a problem with the cornice.

They were right about the board, too. It was three inches too deep. I had not seen the finished board, since it went directly from our workroom to their home. The carpenters thought it was an outside mounted installation instead of an inside mount. I took it down that evening and had it fixed over the weekend. The clients are now thrilled with it and are proceeding to do window treatments in their dining and living rooms.

Your home is one of your biggest investments. Most folks buy new home furnishings only a couple times during their lives. Don't go at it alone; there are wonderful designers that can help you make the most of your home and budget!

Here are some tips for choosing the right designer:

- Be sure the designer you choose is qualified. The American Society of Interior Designers has a referral service by region. Check it out at www.interiors.org.

- Folks with limited budgets need professional help the most because they cannot afford to make mistakes.

- Independently employed designers often charge a per-hour fee.

- Designers employed by a furniture store work on commission. As long as you will be purchasing through the store, their services are free, and they will help you with all the little extras—like picking out paint, even if they don't sell the paint.

- A decorator is not a designer. A designer has a degree; a decorator does not.

Meditations on Bathroom Sanctuaries

PSALM 68:9–10

"You gave abundant showers, O God; you refreshed your weary inheritance. Your people settled in it, and from your bounty, O God, you provided for the poor."

Day 1
I love the thought of water cascading over my body, washing away all dirt and cares.

Day 2
I praise You, Lord, for refreshing waters. Thank You that through Jesus, You have washed away my sins.

Day 3
Thanks for pouring Your bounty on Your people.

Day 4
I pray that You will provide for the poor in my community just as You provided for the Israelites as they wandered in the desert.

Day 5
Sometimes I feel afflicted, like I am in a spiritual desert. Refresh my soul and spirit as I steal a few moments alone with You.

Day 6
May I thrive in Your love. May Your gift of eternal life flow through me and invigorate me like streams of living water.

See photo #1

Bathroom Sanctuaries

The bathroom is not only a room with purpose but also the place where we begin and end our day. And if you have a teenager at home, he or she may have "settled in" your bathroom.

Moms with little ones have bathroom problems too. They rarely get a moment alone—even in the bathroom. Yet a few minutes in the tub can refresh and purify both mind and body.

BEAUTY IS IN

Today's bathrooms are beautiful as well as practical. For many years, they were simply utilitarian. I guess it reflected the state of society—always achieving with no time for peaceful reflection. Oh sure, we wished for those Calgon moments, but we never had time to experience them. But something has changed. Some believe that 9/11 made the difference, but I saw it coming earlier as I worked with clients. We were beginning to recognize that we could not keep our rapid pace. Old biblical ideas were revived even as society rejected the Savior. We needed a Sabbath. We longed for rest, time to recuperate and meditate. Our bathrooms became one of the few spaces where we felt we could close the door and be alone without feeling guilty. Bathrooms began to change and reflect our need for a sanctuary of quiet beauty.

Now some would say bathrooms have gotten too extravagant. Today you can get elaborate style that really works from a mail-order catalog! Consider a fossil-stone top with porcelain sink set into a hardwood chest with silver highlights. It's a mere $1,699 with one sink. For two sinks, you need only $3,999. Laugh as you may, it is a reflection of what is happening and how we are changing.

Your sensory sanctuary can be as simple or intricate as you want it to be. Some choose to create a home spa to retreat to for solace and comfort. Others focus on artistic furnishings or luxurious water delivery. A wet surface lavatory is an example of this. (That's where water flows onto a flat, circular, marble slab that is cut to fit inside the top of the sink bowl. The water hits the smooth marble, which is perpendicular to the water flow, and gently moves over the stone to cascade off the edges into the rest of the bowl that is hidden below.)

BATHS CAN PAMPER

My mother continues the evening ritual she started when her house was full of children. She fills the tub with her favorite scented oils and warm water. Then she soaks for a half hour, giving her body time to relax in the warm water and allowing her mind to drift and find the peace that can only come when we steal away for a few moments with the true Peacemaker.

No matter your budget or the condition of your bathroom, a few simple changes can be enough to pamper the spirit:

ℂ Light a few candles and indulge yourself by purchasing one luxurious towel.

ℂ Place a few plants or flowers in the room to create a garden oasis.

- Add beauty and storage with a small decorative shelf, cabinet, or bench.

- Add detail with crown molding at the ceiling and a frame around your vanity mirror.

- Make an amazing difference with one beautiful rug. I purchased a floral hooked rug that is now the focal point of my bathroom.

- Give a romantic feel to the room with soft shades or pretty hanging glass objects on the window.

- Paste up your favorite colors and pattern by wall-papering the bathroom.

- Stop by your favorite bath and body shop, and treat yourself to a bottle of fragrant bath oil.

Meditations on Fountains and Water

PSALM 36:9

"For with you is the fountain of life; in your light we see light."

Day 1
Thank You, Lord, that You are the Author of everything good and beautiful in life.

Day 2
Help me see life the way You do, having Your eyes and Your perspective.

Day 3
Lead my paths this day and every day with the light of Your presence.

Day 4
Am I drinking enough water from the true spiritual Source?

Day 5
When am I going to other waters for satisfaction and "life" when I ought to go to You?

Day 6
How can I lead others toward the Lord, the fountain of life?

Fountains and Water

I have always loved being near the water. I grew up on Lake Erie, truly a great lake. Even in the midst of a brutal Cleveland winter, I found solace and comfort sitting on the edge of the water. I always felt close to God as I listened to the water wash against the rocks and shore. By focusing on the sound of water, we can block out the unnecessary and inharmonious noises inside our minds, making it possible to hear God's voice. And since God is the creator of water, contemplating it naturally points our thoughts upward. Even today, God often speaks to me during my morning shower. As the warm, soothing water falls, I am open to hearing from my Lord.

ADD A CALMING INFLUENCE

An indoor fountain is an easy way to extend this state of calm throughout your home or office. There are so many wonderful options today (from tabletop styles to freestanding floor models to exquisite wall-mounted works of art) that the hardest part is deciding which you prefer. Tabletop fountains are perfect for the corner of your desk, a bookshelf or nightstand, or your foyer table. Although small, they provide a big sound designed to replicate a country stream or calming pool. It is the simplest way to create a sense of tranquility indoors.

You can choose from a small, decorative fountain to an entire wall of water. A waterfall fountain on the island of Crete inspired one artist, Laura Hansen, to envision wall fountains as works of art. Through Capsis Fountains (see http://cherryorchard.com/falls/capsis-fountains.htm), she has combined dramatic lighting with elegant materials, creating the soothing sound of water flowing over such materials as hardwoods, ceramics, mosaic tile, and glass. This transforms the elements of art and sculpture, as the movement of water over their different shapes creates uniquely beautiful visual delights.

In a sense, the relationship between water and the different shapes in the wall fountains reminds me of the relationship that God has with His people. Jesus Christ is described as living water that revives our parched hearts (John 4:13–14). As the Holy Spirit flows through us and speaks to us, we are transformed, refreshed, and invigorated. He directs our hearts as easily as water runs through an irrigation ditch (Proverbs 21:1). God's gift of new life is the same yesterday, today, and forever; and it is available to all kinds of people, whether they be similar or different shaped "stones" in the house (kingdom) of God.

CHANGE IS NATURAL

We often find ourselves resistant to leaving the limitations of the past and to moving forward to the new life that God wants for us. To watch and hear the flow of water reminds us that flow and change are the natural way of life. Water washes away impurities and carries and deposits nutrients downstream. A fountain can be a reminder of the peace and nourishment we can draw from His strength as we seek to "water" those around us.

For your personal home fountain, here are some things to consider:

- Be sure to choose one with a *quiet* pump. These can be more expensive, but you want to hear the water, not the roar of the motor!

- The best pumps also have a flow adjustment, which allows you to choose how fast your waterfall flows. I prefer a softer, gentler waterfall!

- Use distilled or bottled water for your fountain. Tap water contains calcium, which can eventually solidify in your pump and on your fountain.

- If your fountain begins to smell strange, add a few drops of bleach or vinegar.

- Evaporation is natural. You will need to adjust the level of water to maintain a continuous, quiet, and splash-free operation.

Meditations on Combating Mildew

LEVITICUS 14:35-36

"The owner of the house must go and tell the priest, 'I have seen something that looks like mildew in my house.' The priest is to order the house to be emptied before he goes in to examine the mildew, so that nothing in the house will be pronounced unclean. After this the priest is to go in and inspect the house."

Day 1
Since sin and death entered the world in the garden of Eden, there have been the sorts of things like bacterial growths and infections that are harmful to humankind and the matter around us. Lord, help me not get discouraged or distracted from the important and eternal things while I deal with the troubles and inconveniences that come my way.

Day 2
I can't imagine having to tell a priest about mildew or mold in my house. I think I'd rather call my mother-in-law for help. Thank You, Lord, for little modern conveniences like bleach, which help eradicate the problem.

Day 3
Thank You that You have cleaned out my heart and soul by making me a new creation in Christ.

Day 4
I am glad that You wanted the homes of the Israelites to be clean and free of mildew. That tells me that You care about my home and health too.

Day 5
Is there scum that grows like mildew in my heart?

Day 6
Cleanse me from secret sin and wash me whiter than snow.

Combating Mildew

What's wrong with a little mold and mildew? Why did the Old Testament make such an issue about it? After all, you can hardly see the mold behind the laundry tub. Okay, maybe a little bit is peeking out from behind the wallpaper in the bathroom. Big deal!

A few years ago my sister started noticing black marks on her ceilings. She cleaned them, but they always returned. She had owned her house only a couple of years. The previous owner had installed air-conditioning just prior to selling the home. Who knew that the blessing of air-conditioning would be the cause of my sister's black mold?

She discovered that the contractor never installed a drain for condensation, nor did he ever file a permit for the work. Instead, he took advantage of an elderly homeowner, and now my sister had to pay for it. The EPA deemed her home unlivable. Everything she owned had to be removed, cleaned, or thrown away! But that wasn't the worst of it.

Almost all homeowner insurance policies do *not* cover mold, which left my sister with a mortgage for a home she could not live in or sell. After many months and mountains of frustration, the contractor's insurance company was held liable. But this victory came only after my sister produced health records regarding my niece's cancer history and the fact that both of their pet dogs had lost all their hair since they moved into this home. My sister's home has now been gutted and rebuilt. She was one of the fortunate ones because she eventually got some money toward the repair.

CONQUER AT THE SITE OF THE CAUSE

There are thousands of different types of mold and mildew, but they have two things in common. First, their mission on earth is to digest the organic world around them. Second, they just need a little moisture to work. Not all molds are bad. In fact, without them, our world would be covered with dead trees and plants that would not decay.

The trouble is when it attacks your home. Mold problems and conditions with long-standing moisture or high humidity go hand in hand. To conquer mold, you must also conquer moisture problems that cause it.

Babies and toddlers, who love to crawl around on possibly moldy carpets and stick things in their mouths, are highly vulnerable to mold-induced illnesses. Sensitive adults can develop allergic reactions to mold. Be sure to scrub, dispose, and replace all moldy materials. Most importantly, be sure to dispose of them correctly, or you can make matters worse by sending the spores airborne throughout the house!

Here are some tips for eradicating mold:

- Reduce moisture. I use a dehumidifier in the basement year round.

- Consider purchasing a humidity meter to monitor levels. Humidity should be between 30 and 50 percent.

  Poorly ventilated bathrooms allow surface mold to grow. Remove surface mildew by scrubbing the area with a 50-50 mixture of bleach and water. When the area is dry, prime it with alcohol-based, white-pigmented shellac, such as Zinsser Bull's-eye, and use a paint containing mildewcide.

  Clean bathroom surfaces weekly with a detergent and water solution or a mixture of two cups of distilled vinegar and one-quarter cup of lemon juice in a gallon of water.

  Humidifiers provide both a growth medium and a distribution system for mold and mildew. Clean them frequently.

  Finished concrete basements that haven't been thoroughly waterproofed from the outside allow moisture to get trapped behind the vapor barriers, carpet, insulation, and drywall. If you are having problems, look for obvious solutions, such as cleaning clogged spouts and gutters or covering belowground window wells. However, more complicated measures could be needed, like sloping ground away from the house or installing an interior drainage system.

  Improperly installed, flashed, or caulked windows and exterior finish systems such as Dryvit let moisture seep into and behind the surrounding wood, drywall, and insulation. Have an expert check for existing problems and caulk joints and seams every seven to ten years.

  Wrap pipes in foam to reduce condensation.

  Install storm windows, and wipe panes daily to remove moisture.

Meditations on Divine and Human Plans

PROVERBS 16:9

*"In his heart a man plans his course,
but the LORD determines his steps."*

Day 1
Am I failing to plan or planning too much?

Day 2
What can I do to remember that You are sovereign over all things?

Day 3
Remind me that only those plans that are according to Your will are going to succeed.

Day 4
How can I be more flexible?

Day 5
Help me give thanks for interruptions because You order my steps.

Day 6
Guide me in the way that I should go.

Divine and Human Plans

Have you ever experienced a day when you seemed to accomplish nothing? You started out with a plan and a list, but everything turned to chaos.

Often when I begin working with a new client I feel that way. Yesterday, I had my first meeting with one. Her situation is unique because she has three homes. One is plenty for me, thank you, and I'm a professional interior designer, so I can only imagine how overwhelmed she must feel. One of her homes is a 1740s stone structure in Pennsylvania that must be completely renovated before it is tolerable. The second home is a new one in Florida. It is empty and must be furnished before they can move in. The third home is in Colorado. This is the only home that is livable, although the roof is leaking.

I knew I needed an overall plan to accomplish anything. Before we could begin planning, however, I needed to take time to understand the entire situation. One additional factor that affected our decision making was that this woman's husband broke his back and was incapacitated. His prognosis was uncertain.

We met for nearly an hour before I felt as though we could design a plan of attack. We decided to make furnishing the Florida home a priority. That way, they will have a comfortable place that is safe (because it is all on one floor) for the winter, while we begin renovating the home here in Pennsylvania.

Although this client's situation is atypical, many

clients with redecorating desires start off running in several directions. Attempting to work on several rooms at once usually leaves you with multiple half-done spaces. Don't get me wrong; it is vital to have an overall big picture regarding style, color, and so forth. Attempting to implement it all at once, however, is a nearly impossible feat.

TACKLE ONE SPACE AT A TIME

I learned a long time ago that I am not good at looking for wallpaper for different spaces at the same time. I need to focus on one space and then build on each choice I make. The same is true for our spiritual decisions. Attempting to work on several weak areas at the same time is not as efficient as it sounds.

From experience, I have learned that the Lord convicts me in a specific area at a certain time. That allows me to focus and make the necessary changes. God is so gracious. I know He sees the big picture and all the spiritual growth He wants to make in my life-time, but He doesn't overwhelm me by simultaneous-ly showing me multiple things that need attention. He changes me one area at a time.

When tackling a large project or multiple spaces, it helps to sketch out a master plan. Break the job into smaller parts and then into ordered steps. De-cide which one area is most important for the well-being of your family, and make that the priority. Within that area, designate an order for the jobs that need to be done.

Here are some suggestions for planning your re-modeling project:

⊙ Establish a budget. It may not be easy, but knowing the dollar figure you are comfortable with will provide a good basis. Be specific with what you want, so there are no surprises.

⊙ I suggest two lists: one that details all of your goals and another that addresses specifics such as size and location. Involve the entire family in creating this list of needs and wants.

⊙ Here's the general order of the major components of a remodeling/building project: framing, plumbing, wiring, windows, HVAC, drywall, carpentry finishing, painting, cabinets, hard surface flooring, and carpeting.

⊙ Choose and order all those things that have the longest lead time, such as cabinets, windows, flooring, and countertops.

⊙ Prepare for inconvenience. A remodeling project can turn your home and life upside down. Set up temporary cooking quarters by moving the refrigerator, toaster oven, and microwave to another room.

⊙ Guard against dust. Seal off doorways and stairs with plastic. Turn off central air or heat when workers are sanding, and stock up on extra filters so you can change them often.

⊙ Maintain a sense of humor and consider this a family adventure. One client set up a complete temporary living space in the basement—even the teenage daughters adapted with good spirit!

⊙ Expect delays. Some things are out of your control, like the weather and delays in the arrival of workers or materials.

Meditations on Using Skilled Craftspeople

EXODUS 31:1-6

"Then the LORD said to Moses, 'See I have chosen Bezalel ... and I have filled him with the Spirit of God, with skill, ability and knowledge in all kinds of crafts—to make artistic designs for work in gold, silver and bronze, to cut and set stones, to work in wood.... Moreover, I have appointed Oholiab ... to help him. Also I have given skill to all the craftsmen to make everything I have commanded you.'"

Day 1
God commanded Moses to build the tabernacle and its contents and also gave skills to workers so they could carry out those commands. Thank You, Lord, for being a God who doesn't just command but also equips.

Day 2
I praise You, Lord, for giving some people special skills in using their hands to make beautiful things.

Day 3
How can I better appreciate the beauty of art and skilled work?

Day 4
Help me to respect and encourage the skills of others, including both the craftsperson and his or her helper, knowing that they have been appointed by You.

Day 5
Where can I use the skills and talents you have given me for Your glory?

Day 6
Lead us to people we can serve and to people that can assist us. Help us to be humble and charitable as we give as well as receive from others.

Using Skilled Craftspeople

As a designer, my greatest assets are the skilled craftspeople with whom I work. My team consists of carpenters, plumbers, seamstresses, installers, cabinetmakers, painters and paperhangers, electricians, tile setters, and many other artisans. It takes time and trial and error to gather a good team. We have a mutual respect amongst us and depend on one another to complete projects and refer clients. Our reputation is our calling card. It precedes us, good or bad.

KNOW THE ONE YOU'RE WITH

I know that I can trust every craftsperson within my team. I know they are honest, have proper licensing, insurance, and work ethics, and they will always do the best job possible. They may not be the cheapest, but when it comes to quality, you most often get what you pay for.

I have received too many phone calls from consumers who thought they were getting a good deal only to find that now they must undo a poorly done job. When that happens, they end up spending much more than they would have if they had chosen a quality craftsperson the first time!

Speaking of budgets, always be specific about your needs and your budget when interviewing a perspective craftsperson. Don't pretend to be something you are not. Too often, when interviewing new clients, I feel as though they are trying to impress me. As a result, they are not completely honest about their needs and lifestyle. Designers, architects, and carpenters are just like you. We have families, we watch TV, our kids track mud through the house, and we leave the ironing board up in the bedroom. We understand and want to solve your home problems in a way that will make sense for you, your family, and your budget.

WHERE TO LOOK

When it comes to locating qualified and trustworthy contractors, ask for recommendations from folks like myself or your friends, neighbors, and family members. The Better Business Bureau (BBB) can give you a list of local members, as can the Building Industry Association. Ultimately, you should interview and check references of anyone you are considering.

One of the key points to consider is whether or not you have compatible personalities. No matter how accomplished a craftsperson is, if you do not like him or her, you will never be pleased. Interview at least three different people. When calling to set up an interview, ask how large or small a project they usually consider. Also, be sure they specialize in residential construction and home improvement.

Here are some basic questions to ask a skilled craftsperson when interviewing them:

- How do you determine your fee schedule? Is it flexible?

- How long have you been involved in renovation? Do you have a portfolio?

- Has a client ever brought suit against you? If so, why, and how was it resolved?

❧ Will you provide in writing all products specified, including brands and model numbers, so I know exactly what I am getting?

❧ Does your contract provide for conflict resolution? If so, how? (Mediation is my first choice if you cannot work it out yourselves.)

❧ Will you contract a finish date?

❧ Discuss liability issues and ask for copies of their insurance coverage. Consider having an attorney check it to be sure it is adequate.

❧ Are you a member of the BBB? If not, why not?

❧ Do you use subcontractors? If so, may I have their names and references? Oftentimes, the price and quality of the subcontractors employed determine the price and quality of your job.

❧ Discuss job maintenance. Maintaining a clean, organized site is imperative to a well-executed job.

❧ Who will be responsible for obtaining necessary permits, inspections, filings, and engineering? Are the fees associated included in the contract?

❧ And, last but not least, remember that it is your home, and you are in charge of the job!

Meditations on Designs for Caregiving

JOHN 19:26-27

"When Jesus saw his mother there, and the disciple whom he loved standing nearby [His cross], he said to his mother, 'Dear woman, here is your son,' and to the disciple, 'Here is your mother.' From that time on, this disciple took her into his home."

Day 1
Thank You, Jesus, for caring about Your family and friends even while You were hanging on the cross.

Day 2
How wonderful to know that I can be a disciple or friend whom Jesus loves!

Day 3
Thank You for Your love, the love of others, and for giving me a place to call home.

Day 4
Help me to remember that having a special position of love often brings with it a position of increased responsibility.

Day 5
Who is standing nearby in my sphere of responsibility or influence?

Day 6
Do You want me to bring someone into my home?

Designs for Caregiving

One of the biggest issues of our time is simultaneously managing the care of our children and our aging parents. Recent research shows that this trend is likely to continue. A study by the American Association of Retired Persons found that 83 percent of respondents want to remain in their current residence as long as possible.[1] The problem is that their homes are not designed for them to do that safely. My parents are a typical case study. My dad had multiple sclerosis. He had been in a wheelchair for four or five years. As his health continued to deteriorate, his care became increasingly difficult. My siblings and I encouraged Mom to think about putting Dad in a nursing home, fearing she was risking her own health in caring for him. Neither she nor Dad would consider it.

My mom wanted to care for my dad because when her own father's health was failing, my father became his caregiver. That was amazing, because my grandfather and father had been rivals for decades. After Grandpa moved in, it became obvious that it was emotionally too difficult for my mother to care for him. We all watched in amazement as my father took over more of the care—feeding, bathing, cheering up, and challenging Grandpa with love, affection, and a good sense of humor. Dad and Grandpa became best friends.

Mom felt it was her turn to repay the favor, so my siblings and I made changes throughout their house to accommodate Dad's needs. We held family celebrations at their home, or at least chose places that could accommodate Dad's wheelchair. My youngest brother, who was single, moved in with my parents. His strong arms lifted Dad, and he took on the weekly grocery shopping as well as the yard care. Of course, Mom was soon back to spoiling her youngest child and loving it.

EVALUATE THE HOME AND INDIVIDUAL NEEDS

For older people with health problems, a home evaluation by an occupational therapist can be helpful. My parents had a representative from the MS Society inspect their home. The suggestions the inspector made were wonderful because they were specific to my father's needs. Other ailments such as arthritis require special adaptations; for example, replacing doorknobs and faucets with lever handles. Other ideas include installing an under-cabinet jar opener or electric can opener.

Don't forget to provide transportation for aging loved ones to exercise classes, grocery shopping, and social events. Encourage them to get out of the house and to maintain their friendships.

Here is a basic checklist for making a home more accessible to the ill or disabled:

- Install securely fastened handrails on both sides of all stairways.

- Make sure all areas, including stairways, are well lit.

- Have a telephone in easily accessible places in all major rooms.

- Remove or anchor throw rugs and clear traffic areas of cords.

- Install bars that can be held onto in the tub, shower, and near the toilet. Be sure they are anchored properly.

- Install a seat and nonslip surface to the tub.

- Be vigilant whenever a handicapped person under your care takes a bath. Ensure they do not scald themselves with hot water.

- Put a fire extinguisher within easy reach of the stove.

- Install automatic nightlights throughout the home.

- Keep frequently used items within easy reach without the use of a chair or stool.

- Install and regularly inspect smoke detectors and carbon monoxide detectors.

NOTE

1. Gibson, Mary Jo and others, eds,. "Physical Environment and Independence," *Beyond 50.03: A Report to the Nation on Independant Living and Disability* (Washington D.C.: AARP, 2003), 91. See http://research.aarp.org/il/beyond_50_il_1.html

Meditations on Creativity

2 CORINTHIANS 5:17

*"Therefore, if anyone is in Christ, he is a new creation;
the old has gone, the new has come!"*

Day 1
I praise You, Lord, for being the author of creativity.

Day 2
Thank You for giving Christ, Your only Son, to die for my sins so that I can
be a new creation.

Day 3
Forgive me for allowing old habits and sin patterns to poke through my
new life in You.

Day 4
How can I keep my old nature from hijacking my attitudes and behavior?

Day 5
Help me view others as You see them, as new creations, and to love them.

Day 6
What can I do to become a spiritually mature new creation?

Creativity

live in central Pennsylvania, which is known as the Antique Capital of the World. People come from all over the East Coast to shop for bargains. My husband and I are both caught up in the thrill of the "hunt."

For example, picture and mirror frames have become popular. Entire catalogs are dedicated to just this one home-decorating product. Of course, with demand comes an increase in price and value. Some of these frames cost hundreds of dollars, so shopping at flea markets for old frames is one way to get the best of both price and style. A little creativity is all you need.

ONE WOMAN'S TRASH IS ANOTHER WOMAN'S TREASURE

Recently, I bargained for a 1970s-era Mediterranean picture frame. I found it under a table at a local shop. When I asked the price, the proprietor responded, "With or without the dust?" Six dollars later, I walked away with a one-of-a-kind treasure.

My six-dollar frame is now a beautiful "gold-leaf" frame. When I say "gold-leaf," I mean real leaves! After washing the dirt off the frame, I decorated it by attaching gold-painted, dried leaves and berries. The richness of the finished frame is elegant with a three-dimensional look that is delicate yet makes a strong and beautiful statement on the wall.

Crafting comes naturally to me, but that is not true for everyone. I have done a lot of craft projects for television. Often, the hosts of the shows will comment on how they could never make or do such crafts. In most cases, it's just a matter of getting started. Everyone has creative ability. They just express it differently according to their own thinking styles.

ARE YOU AN ADAPTER OR AN INNOVATOR?

I recently took a test on creativity by a group that is researching the creative process. According to their findings, thinking style is an inherited personality characteristic that influences where people go for information, how they sort the information, and how they use it. They divided people into two groups: adapters and innovators. Adapters are comfortable in structured environments and with established ways of doing things. Innovators are the opposite. They feel comfortable with incomplete information and little structure. Regardless, both types of people are capable of creative thinking and activity. It's just a matter of choosing the right project for their thinking processes.

If you are an adapter, go ahead and start a craft project based on someone else's idea. Purchase a pattern to knit or sew, or craft something from a kit. If you are an innovator, then design a new sweater pattern for your child. When my nieces and nephews were young, each year we would sit down and design a sweater together. Then I would knit it for them. They learned how to be creative in the process and got the bonus of a new, one-of-a-kind sweater.

God is both an adapter who makes new beings out of old sinners and an innovator who spoke the heavens and the earth into being by the power of His voice (Genesis 1).

Here are some questions from CIM Testing to help you determine your creative thinking process:

> ☙ Do you like to find new ways of doing things? If so, then give yourself a point as an innovator.

> ☙ Do you let others do most of the talking? If true, then you get one point as an adapter.

> ☙ Are you willing to take calculated risks? This is another sign of innovation.

> ☙ Have you gotten set in your ways? If so, then you are setting up camp with the adapters.

> ☙ Have you sat back in a group and wished you could express yourself, but didn't? If the answer is yes, that's another point on the adapter side.

> ☙ Do you keep up with new technology? If so, that's a sure sign of innovation.

> ☙ Do you love interacting with your children? That's a sign that it's time to start a family craft project. Whether you're adapting or innovating, just have fun!

Meditations on Teamwork

PROVERBS 4:1-2 KJV

"Hear, ye children, the instruction of a father, and attend to know understanding. For I give you good doctrine, forsake ye not my law."

Day 1
Lord, thank You for the blessing of parents and families.

Day 2
Grant me wisdom as I train my children in godly living.

Day 3
Help my children and other young ones in my circle of influence to prick up their ears whenever I talk of spiritual things.

Day 4
Grant discernment and godly perception to my children.

Day 5
What good doctrine can I teach someone today, and how should I impart it?

Day 6
Help me not to forsake the great lessons that my parents and leaders taught me, and help me pass their legacy on to others.

Teamwork

Proverbs 4 focuses on the importance of wisdom. *Attend* means prick up your ears like an animal. The word *know* can mean perceive or discern in the moral sense or knowledge gained through the senses, including technical skills. The imparting of wisdom between adult and child is like a dance. It's an art with each person playing a part. We don't always have to talk to teach. One of the easiest ways to teach someone both technical skills and moral wisdom is demonstration. Start by showing them basic skills, and then allow them to build on each new skill as their confidence grows.

BARNS AND WATER GARDENS LEAD TO CONFIDENCE

This summer I witnessed two families enjoying the results of such teaching and teamwork. Over the last ten years, one family built an amazing garden and water retreat in their backyard. A fountain feeds a manmade stream, directing water through ponds, gardens, a beach area—complete with sand and beach chairs alongside a mini-lake—and ending at an ingenious system for watering their vegetable garden. Along this path are gardens, gazebos, a tree, which has been forced to create a chair within its split branches, and a covered deck.

Under Dad's supervision, this family's three children, two sons ages thirteen and fifteen and an eleven-year-old daughter, designed and built an incredible small barn. It is artistic, fun, and functional, with double doors and a banked ramp for driving the tractor in and out. What an accomplishment for these children! The family allowed the community to visit this special place when they opened their home for the garden tour. Their garden and barn are testimonies to what can be accomplished if people work together. The confidence gained through this experience will help these children tackle life with a positive attitude.

A NEW DECK BRINGS A SENSE OF BELONGING

The second family also has two sons and a daughter. The boys, ages fourteen and eighteen, and the daughter, age ten, designed, ordered supplies, and built a new deck for the family home. It, too, is far beyond most adults' expectations or abilities. These families model perseverance, teamwork, and disciple making.

If families work together as a team, our homes are easier to maintain, and renovation projects become bonding and confidence-building experiences that result in feelings of belonging and accomplishment for everyone. In addition, new brain research shows that children need a sense of connectedness to thrive.

While each of us has certain abilities, all of us can learn some new skills with the right attitude. I may never make my living as a portrait painter, but I can still enjoy the process of learning basic painting skills. It is the process that is good for me. Both our moral and technical training is experienced through the senses. Our homes, like us, are ongoing processes, growing and changing as we move to meet the next challenges in our changing families.

Many hands make light work. Here are some tips for working together as a family team:

- Lay the foundation before you begin construction. Provide the vision and leadership. The most successful teams invest time in determining who will do what to create a common framework for everyone. Set realistic goals.

- Provide specific instruction in a way that kids can understand. Divide jobs into smaller steps for younger children. Allow older ones to experiment with ordering their courses of action. Ask your children to "report in" after they've completed a job. Be available to offer support and encouragement. Everyone responds better when treated respectfully.

- Celebrate the work and its completion. Don't forget to tell each one how much you appreciate his or her part.

- Volunteering is a great way to bring people together. You can rally your neighbors to clean up that vacant lot on the corner or paint an elderly neighbor's house.

- Consider the skills you have to offer. If you enjoy outdoor work, have a knack for teaching, or just enjoy people, look for volunteer work that incorporates these aspects of your personality.

- Find a volunteer opportunity suitable for the whole family to do together. The experience can bring you closer together, teach young children the value of giving their time and effort, and introduce the family to new skills and experiences.

Meditations on Preparing Your Home for Winter

MATTHEW 6:19-20

"Do not store up for yourselves treasures on earth, where moth and rust destroy, and where thieves break in and steal. But store up for yourselves treasures in heaven, where moth and rust do not destroy, and where thieves do not break in and steal."

Day 1
What a reminder that we live in a fallen world!

Day 2
Am I holding on to this world and my possessions too tightly?

Day 3
What are my treasures, and where am I storing them?

Day 4
Lord, grant me balance as I strive to take care of my home without loving it too much.

Day 5
What can I do today to store up eternal treasures?

Day 6
May I stand before God one day blameless and holy because I have stored up treasures in heaven.

Preparing Your Home for Winter

A house is an earthly investment. Although we don't like to admit it, earthly possessions don't last. No matter how well we maintain the exterior of our homes, every five to twenty years, things deteriorate and must be repainted, resurfaced, or reroofed. Performing a few quick and easy maintenance chores around your home can save you time and money later.

PERFORM AN OUTDOOR INSPECTION

Walk around the outside of your home. Inspect the foundation for cracks. Repair them using heavy caulk or ready-mix cement. This will prevent cold air from seeping into your home and save you money in energy costs. Inspect the condition of your exterior paint. If it has been four years since your home has been painted, call your painter in the fall to get on his or her list for the spring season. Everyone calls during the first pleasant week in spring, so you risk being buried in the avalanche. Beat the rush, get more personalized service, and bless your painters. Winter is a slow season for them, so having your job to look forward to in the spring can give them and their families a morale boost.

MAKE CHANGES TO YOUR INTERIOR

I am always looking for attractive ways to winterize a home. In the spring, we have the need to clean house, get rid of excess, open up the spaces, and let in the light. The opposite is true for winter. Suddenly, we'll feel the urge to fill our spaces. I call this the nesting syndrome. The open, light-colored spaces feel too cool. Colors affect our emotional well-being. We seek warmth in winter, and the right color can actually make us feel better. It's natural to add warmer colors as winter sets in. I like to change to warmer colors, especially in my bedroom. You can do this by using different bedclothes, draperies, and accessories.

Don't forget to clean the heating ducts and vents throughout your home. This will not only insure there are no blockages but also increase the efficiency of your furnace. As an added benefit, you'll have a cleaner home. This cleaning should be done at least once every five years. Another way to keep warm air from escaping your home is to install a door sweep to the bottom of your doors. To prevent further drafts, try using a door pillow. You can make one to match your décor! The most usable size is approximately two to three inches high by thirty-six inches long. Consider using a quilt as a wall hanging to hang over a patio door. It's a beautiful way to insulate a cold wall or doorway!

Many of the newer homes have an abundance of windows. They allow natural heat in during sunny days. At night, however, they can become cold-air monsters! To provide a simple nighttime solution for large windows, cut insulation foam to sizes slightly larger than your window. At night put the pieces in the window to keep cold air out and remove them in the morning to let the sunshine in. (Egg crate foam works well.) To insulate a drafty attic door, staple a sheet of insulation foam to the back of it.

Here are some tips for warming up your nest for winter:

- Turn the direction of heating vents from up to down because hot air always rises. Have your furnace or heat pump checked. Make sure the furnace filter is clean. Check the thermostat to be sure it is working properly and the pilot light is functioning.

- Check your chimney. I have mine professionally cleaned each year. Consider installing a screen over your chimney opening.

- Clean your gutters and ridge vents. If clogged, rainwater backs up and if the temperature drops below freezing, the standing water freezes, causing the gutters to expand and crack.

- Make sure your smoke alarm and carbon monoxide detectors are working, and install fresh batteries.

- Check the caulking around your doors and windows to be sure it is not cracked or peeling, which will allow your home's heat to escape.

- Put away garden hoses. Insulate exterior spigots. Drain and shut off sprinkler systems and other exterior water lines to avoid frozen and broken pipes.

- Seal driveway and walkway cracks, if needed, before the ground freezes.

Meditations on Happy Hideaways

MATTHEW 14:23

"After [Jesus] had dismissed [the crowd], he went
up on a mountainside by himself to pray.
When evening came, he was there alone."

Day 1
I love knowing that Jesus, though perfect, needed to get away from the crowds and be alone.

Day 2
Lord, I come to You now, seeking to close the door on the world and my worries in order to pray.

Day 3
Do I have crowds I need to dismiss? What are my crowds? Too much TV? Too much people pleasing? Too many selfish wants?

Day 4
When evening comes and I am alone, will I be afraid or will I be prepared for Christ's next great act?

Day 5
Enable me to honor and focus on You, Lord, even when no one is looking.

Day 6
How can I make a place, a sanctuary, in which to pray?

Happy Hideaways

One of my favorite childhood memories is of the entire family playing hide-and-seek. Mom dimmed the lights throughout the house, Dad put on some appropriately eerie music, and the fun began. The older children helped to hide the younger ones. As the oldest of six children, I loved the challenge of hiding my youngest sister somewhere that neither my siblings nor my parents could find.

As we huddled in the dark, our anticipation grew. The younger children sometimes got scared while they waited. The better the hiding place, the longer it took to be found, and the more their realization grew that they were alone in the dark. Their emotions moved from anxious delight to fear and back again.

Shrieks of joy erupted as each child was found. Once found, we became part of the search party. On and on it went, searching inside cupboards, up on rafters, and even in the china cabinet, until the last one was found. With each new generation, the game has continued. It is even better now because we get to play in several houses, which creates a new challenge every time.

I recently read about a new book by Katrina Kenison called *Mitten Strings for God*, which talks about children's need for secret hideaways. She calls it the human need for sanctuary. A mother in Wichita, Kansas, says her seven-year-old daughter likes to climb into a cabinet in the kitchen. She squeezes her wiry body inside and turns on her flashlight. Sometimes she reads a book. Other times, she colors. The point is that she loves it in there.

SANCTUARY NEEDS

We all need a place of sanctuary, a place where we can hide and be alone and have the opportunity to relax and reconnect with God. With the hectic pace of today's lifestyles, finding and creating sanctuaries within our homes for each family member is important. It also means we must respect one another's right to uninterrupted time alone. Going to our hideaway should be a signal to the rest of the family that we don't want to be disturbed.

As a child, my hideaway changed from my playhouse, to a tree, and finally to the attic. The attic was the one place the younger children did not want to be, which made it perfect for me. There I read, wrote, prayed, studied, and cried. No matter the weather—heat of summer or cold of winter—it was my place.

Help your family members create personal hideaways with these tips:

- Enlist your children in a search for their own personal place. Remember that they have a different perspective than do you.

- Tree houses are favorites. My neighbor just built a log-cabin tree house, complete with porch and wooden lounge chairs. His kids love it!

- Gardens are another great place to create a hideaway. One friend has a secret garden just for children. It is filled with whimsical characters and secret messages for the kids.

◈ Use the nooks and crannies of your home. A niche or dormer can be a great place for reading, knitting, listening to music, or just sitting. Don't be afraid to use an overstuffed chair in a small space, just place it on a diagonal and it will fool the eye into thinking the space is larger than it is.

◈ Hang a curtain to separate a corner or niche from the rest of the space. A simple tieback can allow you to open or close the space, or you could use a folding screen.

◈ Carve out a hideaway under a staircase. You will be amazed at how much room you can find there.

Meditations on a Proper Place for Possessions

PROVERBS 15:16

*"Better is a little with the fear of the LORD
than great wealth with turmoil."*

Day 1
You are a God of justice and love. You see all my actions and attitudes.
I praise you!

Day 2
Show me what it means to fear and reverence You.

Day 3
Am I truly content?

Day 4
Lord, take away my desire to amass wealth and possessions.

Day 5
How can I live in a way that shows that spiritual things are more
important than physical wealth?

Day 6
How have I created turmoil in my house by having too many things and
loving them too much?

A Proper Place for Possessions

I recently watched a television interview between a therapist and a patient who was a pack rat. The patient even admitted to hoarding the shards of glass from a broken dish! The therapist tried to get at the root of this problematic desire to hoard things. Ultimately, the therapist decided that this nervous but happy patient was insecure, and this was causing him to be a pack rat.

ADDITIONS FOR ADDITIONAL STUFF

I'm not so sure about the diagnosis of insecurity, but I have certainly seen my share of pack rats. Sam and Claire come to mind. They have lived in the same house for twenty-five years.

About ten years ago, they built an addition, which allowed them to enlarge their master bedroom and bathroom and add a music room for Claire. Family treasures are important to them. As furniture, photos, dishes, accessories, rugs, and other items from both sides of the family began appearing, they felt they had to keep them. Each year, more things arrived. I thought we would have to build another addition.

Unfortunately, a fire destroyed two-thirds of their house. No one was home and no one was hurt, but the floors tumbled in on themselves, landing in the basement. They cried as we walked through the rubble, but they rejoiced at every found candleholder or salvageable photograph. After much consideration, they decided to rebuild.

UNPACKING THE PACK RAT

Since rebuilding, their children grew up and moved out, and now they are ready to build what they expect to be their last home. We laughed as we discussed what would be moved to the new home and what would be sold or passed on to the younger generation of pack rats. Sam said he was ready to let go of things. Claire retorted that she was *not* ready. She needed her clutter. Sam laughed and told her he would build a room in the new home where she could keep all her clutter together. "Whenever you feel the need," Sam said, "you can go sit in there with your stuff!"

Sam's desire to simplify his life and home is something we all strive for, but getting there is a tough process. Just finding the time to sort through things it hard enough, not to mention the emotional toll of evaluating sentimental shreds of earlier days and deciding to toss them. Some people move every couple of years just to clean out their accumulated "treasures."

Here are some tips to simplify your home without going to such an extreme:

- Set small goals. The thought of uncluttering an entire home at once is overwhelming.

- Choose a time to start going through each room and deciding what to keep, throw away, or donate to charity.

- Start in one section of your home and keep moving until you are finished. Each week eliminate something.

- Get rid of any items you have not used in a year.

- If you have things in storage or in boxes that you haven't missed since you moved in, throw them out without opening them.

- Keep only those things that you truly love or really need.

- If you can't decide whether or not to keep an item, ask your best friend to give you an honest answer.

- Think twice before buying anything new. Be sure you have a use for it.

- Enjoy your new uncluttered look. The best design plan leaves room for future treasures.

Meditations on a Moving Experience

JOHN 14:2-3

"In my Father's house are many rooms; if it were not so, I would have told you. I am going there to prepare a place for you. And if I go and prepare a place for you, I will come back and take you to be with me that you also may be where I am."

Day 1
How comforting to know my heavenly Father has a house with many rooms. His house must be grand, spacious, and airy to accommodate a multitude.

Day 2
I praise You, Lord, for being an honest, trustworthy God. I can depend on You to tell me the truth about things to come.

Day 3
I feel special because You are preparing a place just for me. I wonder what types of preparations need to be made. Will they be finished soon?

Day 4
Some days, Lord, I want to escape this life. I want You to take me away to be with You immediately. Other days, I want You to tarry for years. Thank You for doing what's best for everyone and not acting on our whims.

Day 5
Thank You for this promise that You will come and take me to be with You. I long for that day and thank You that I don't have to pack boxes to get ready.

Day 6
Prepare me for life with You.

A Moving Experience

Moving is one of the three most traumatic experiences of life—right up there with death and divorce. Even if you want to move and are looking forward to a new home, it is still stressful. When we consider that 43 million Americans—that's one in six —move per year, we are talking about a lot of stressed-out people! Perhaps even thinking about moving to heaven creates stress for some. God may have all the preparations ready, but we can't get our minds around the forever of eternity and brevity of this life.

Moves often occur when a husband is transferred. The man will visit the area first, scout out the community, and sometimes purchase a home or lease an apartment that he thinks is right for his family. Unfortunately, as many of us know, men do not look at homes the same way women do! Many not-so-happy surprises occur when wives get their first glimpses of their new homes.

EMERGENCY CALL

A number of years ago, I received a phone call at 6:30 A.M. from a real estate colleague. He had sold a typical two-story colonial-style home in Pennsylvania to a husband from California. The wife had arrived the evening before to see the new home. With tears of dismay, she said she could not live in this outdated pioneer home! It didn't even have a fireplace in the master bedroom! My colleague wanted me to come and save the day.

A few hours later, I met the unhappy couple. Fortunately, the house was still under construction. With compassion and empathy I listened to the wife pour out her heart. She had spent the last two months in California alone with the children while she prepared for the sale of their old home and the cross-country move. Upon arriving in Pennsylvania, she began to realize just how different their lives would be. The style of the home was the final blow. Suddenly, something as silly as a fireplace in the master bedroom became hugely important.

WARMING UP

As we stood on the second floor in the soon-to-be-finished master bedroom, I stuck my head out the opening where a window soon would be. I spotted the mason. He was preparing to brick up the chimney. "Hold on a second!" I hollered down to him. "We need to add a fireplace right here, between these two windows in the master bedroom." That was just the beginning of my challenge to turn an East Coast Colonial into a California Suite.

The California-native family lived there for three years. Since then, the home has been sold twice. Dear clients of mine now live there with their family of four. And guess what? The house is back to its old, colonial-style roots, but it still has a fireplace in the master bedroom!

Here are some tips for making your earthly moves a little easier:

⌒ As soon as possible, sort, weed out, and pack up seasonal items you won't need.

- Find a reputable and well-insured mover six to eight weeks before moving.

- Obtain copies of medical, dental, school, and veterinarian records to take with you.

- Cancel newspapers, garbage collection, and lawn services. Arrange to have all utilities and other services such as Internet and cable terminated the day after you move. Schedule their start date in your new home.

- Close out or transfer your bank accounts to your new location.

- Gather all your valuables, jewelry, and important papers to take with you personally.

- Pack a box of valuables for each of your children. Let them decide what must go in this box, so you won't have to spend your first night looking for your child's favorite sleeping "companion."

- Get a change-of-address kit from the post office.

- Pack a box of essentials. Include toilet paper, soap, toothbrushes, hair dryer, paper towels, garbage bags, paper plates and cups, radio, flashlight, and lightbulbs.

- Draw floor plans showing where your furniture should be placed. This will make the movers' (and your) job much less confusing,

- Enlist your best friends to help with all of the above.

- Bring your sense of humor. Everything goes better with a good attitude.

Meditations on Wonderful Window Treatments

JOSHUA 2:12, 17–18, 21

"'Please swear to me by the LORD that you will show kindness to my family, because I have shown kindness to you. Give me a sure sign.'… The men said to her, 'This oath you made us swear will not be binding on us unless, when we enter the land, you have tied this scarlet cord in the window through which you let us down.'… So she sent them away and they departed. And she tied the scarlet cord in the window."

Day 1
The story of Rahab and the spies amazes me. What made Joshua and Caleb trust a prostitute? Did they stay up late at night, talking about God?

Day 2
Rahab is listed in the Bible's Hall of Fame in Hebrews 11 and named in James 2:22–26 as someone whose faith took action. Do I have heroic faith?

Day 3
When I think of Rahab's past and her sinful life, I feel encouraged that God can forgive me too. How has God helped me overcome my past?

Day 4
How many times did Rahab look out her window, longing for the day when she would be saved out of Jericho?

Day 5
Who made the red cord? Did she check it every night before retiring and every morning upon awakening? That cord marked her salvation. And it foreshadowed Jesus' blood shed for sins.

Day 6
Lord, may I be a woman of faith who longingly looks for Your promised return.

Wonderful Window Treatments

I've always wondered if the other women in Jericho thought Rahab was starting a new window treatment fad when she dangled that red cord outside her window. She was a city prostitute, so perhaps they ignored her strange action. If this scarlet cord was the rope she used to help Joshua and Caleb escape the city, then it was a perfect blend of function and creativity.

NEW IDEAS FOR YOUR WINDOWS!

Every year the International Window Coverings Show is held in Baltimore, Maryland. After attending, I always come back energized! Today's window fashions feature layer upon layer of pattern, texture, detail, and color—lots of color! It is the fusion of creativity and function that makes these elements come together for the best window treatments.

Whether we realize it or not, windows are an important architectural feature in a room. Dressing them requires a two-step process. First, you must decide whether or not a particular window needs to be privatized. In other words, will you need to cover it completely for privacy or sleeping? Second, you need to decide if you want a hard or soft treatment.

Hard window treatments are the functional portion of a window treatment, such as shades, blinds, or shutters. One type of hard treatments actually looks *soft*. Luminette window shadings combine the function of blinds with the beauty of sheer draperies. Vertical, translucent fabric slats hang from facings at the top of the window. By rotating the slats from completely opened to completely closed, or any increment in between, you'll enjoy varied levels of light and privacy. You can draw the sheers closed for gently diffused light, or open them and pull them to the sides like curtains for unobstructed views. For contemporary rooms they are great on their own. For more traditional rooms, you can combine them with other soft treatments.

Soft treatments are what you probably think of as curtains or draperies. Today's soft treatments also encompass cornice boards, valances, roman shades, balloon shades, swags and jabots, and, of course, side panels—just to name a few.

LET CREATIVITY REIGN

Designing window treatments is one of the most creative areas of my job. More and more, it is becoming a bigger part of my work. For much of my career, windows didn't get the attention they deserved. Now, as society is digging in and planting roots, windows are blossoming into showcases.

Here are some ideas to get your creativity started:

> ✒ Whether your preference is layers upon layers or just a little softening around the edges, fabric is the most critical element to consider. Price, durability, and its draping quality will all affect the outcome of your window treatment.

> ✒ Today's fabrics are lush and amazing. The most popular fabric is silk. It's available in every color and weave imaginable, and the best part is that silk is more affordable than ever.

◌ Today's sheer fabrics are both fun and sophisticated. One of my favorites has feathers woven sporadically throughout!

◌ Trims such as cording and tassels can add an elegant touch. Maybe a designer somewhere was inspired by Rahab's red cord. Whether you prefer traditional or contemporary, there is a trim to fit your style.

◌ Drapery hardware can give a window that *wow* factor. There is a proliferation of decorative drapery hardware in many materials for self-expression—everything from classic woods to sumptuous crystal in amazing finishes. Glass, bamboo, leather, wrought iron, stainless steel, gold leaf, and brushed aluminum are just some of the materials now available. No more hiding—today's drapery rods demand attention.

◌ Hard window coverings such as shades and shutters are also bigger and better. Wonderful woven grasses and reeds combined with fabric trims create a natural look for controlling light. Wood, fabric, or metal blinds and shutters provide an abundance of choices for shading. And almost any window treatment can be operated by remote control!

◌ Gorgeous window treatments require skilled hands and creative designers. Don't risk your beautiful fabric to an amateur or you will be penny-wise, but dollar-foolish.

Meditations on Accessories

ECCLESIASTES 8:15

"So I commend the enjoyment of life, because nothing is better for a man under the sun than to eat and drink and be glad. Then joy will accompany him in his work all the days of the life God has given him under the sun."

Day 1
Father, it is so easy to go about my duties without joy. Forgive me.

Day 2
Grant my family and me the ability to wear the joy of life as jewelry.

Day 3
Thank You for food and drink and work.

Day 4
Thank You for the days of my life—however many they may be.

Day 5
Let my home and everything in it shine with the accessory of joy.

Day 6
What spots in my home and what attitudes in my heart could use accessories of joy?

See photo #6

Accessories

Accessories are your home's jewelry. The word "accessory" means an object of secondary importance that adds beauty or convenience: artwork, books, plants, photos, sculptures, flowers, cups, baskets, magazines, dishes, pillows, afghans, teapots, a vase, even stationery. Just for a moment, imagine how beautiful your home looks when decorated for the holidays. Now imagine how bare your holiday home would be without any accessories.

TELL YOUR STORY WITH ACCESSORIES

I believe that the items we display around our homes should tell the story of our lives and add a sense of joy. Pictures of family and friends, found treasures that washed up on shore where you vacationed, or even a favorite book—each of these tells a chapter of your life.

These items are special not only to us but also to those around us. I cannot imagine my mother's home without the photos of her great-grandchildren and grandchildren displayed throughout it. Recently, while visiting a client for the first time, I remarked on the lack of photos. She said some designer had told her it was inappropriate for family photos to be displayed in the "public" rooms of the house. I never considered a home to be a public building. I quickly dispelled that myth, and we began choosing areas throughout her home for all her important family pictures.

Most of the work I do with clients involves accessorizing their home. Many folks feel confident in choosing the big items, like sofas and chairs, but get nervous about the little items. Some of those beautiful magazine photos of "dream" homes and rooms can be intimidating.

BEGIN DRESSING FROM A CLEAN SPACE

When I start working with a client on this, I have them remove all accessories from the room. I also have them pull out and clean all their important treasures and place them in one spot so I can work from there. Then, slowly, one item at a time, I begin the "dressing" of the spaces within the room. I caution clients that we probably won't use everything. I gave one client guilt-free permission to pack away at least half of what she owned and told her to save it for future generations. There was just no way we could use all of her collected items in one home!

How you use your accessories separates the dust catchers from the sensational. Here are some tips:

- Start with your largest or tallest item, and then add items of declining height. Never attempt to have two items as focal points.

- When working with symmetrical spaces, use symmetrical accessories. Color and texture will affect the composition. The darker the color or the heavier the texture, the more visual weight an item or wall has. Never use small, delicate items against strong colors or walls.

- Balance vertical elements with horizontal elements. Use diagonals in composition to create an illusion that the eye perceives as more space. This is great for smaller spaces.

⊘ Use larger artwork on smaller walls to create the illusion of a larger space. But never use small artwork on a large wall.

⊘ Analyze your personal style. Is your preference abstract? Use a combination of small and large accessories. Do you like a cleaner, sparser look? Then stay with large accessories. Leave about 12 inches of breathing space around each one.

⊘ Try to use at least one item that is organic in nature.

⊘ In a hallway, hang wall decorations so the midpoint is at standing-eye height: five to six feet high. In a dining or living room, art should be closer to seated-eye level. Artwork should be hung three to four inches above the furniture to avoid UFOs: Unidentified Floating Objects.

Meditations on Decorating with Mirrors

1 CORINTHIANS 13:12

"Now we see but a poor reflection as in a mirror; then we shall see face to face. Now I know in part; then I shall know fully, even as I am fully known."

Day 1
Imagining Christ with my puny brain is like looking at my reflection in a polished piece of metal. I see only some of what's there.

Day 2
Lord, remind me that the beauty of reflections on earth is nothing compared to the beauty I'll see in heaven.

Day 3
Now I know about God from reading His Word. Someday I'll know Him face-to-face.

Day 4
What must I do to be ready for that day?

Day 5
Do I reflect Christ on a daily basis?

Day 6
How can I allow the Holy Spirit to polish and expand my spiritual mirrors?

Decorating with Mirrors

A year ago, my sister was visiting my home. We were standing in front of the full-length mirror in my dressing area when she frowned and said, "This is a *fat* mirror!"

"What do you mean?" I asked.

"This mirror makes me look fatter than I am."

I was sure my mirror was of good quality and that the reflection we were seeing was accurate, so I said nothing. The next time I visited my sister, I made a point to look at myself in her bedroom mirror. I was thrilled to see a *thin* Sharon! After seeing herself in the photos from a recent wedding, my sister began to accept that she was heavier than she thought. Her skinny mirror had hidden the truth of her weight gain. Now, several months and a gym membership later, she is a thinner and healthier sister.

USE A GOOD QUALITY MIRROR

Often we see ourselves only through the reflection of our own eyes, which can give a false impression of the reality. When we look into God's Word, our spiritual reflection is of good quality as we allow the Holy Spirit to quicken our conscience. It's important to use good quality physical and spiritual mirrors.

One of my clients experienced a different problem with mirrors. I recommended one above her family room fireplace. Her budget was tight, so she went to a local home décor store and thought she got a great bargain when she found a large beautifully framed mirror at a small price. A few days later she called me to look at it, asking if I could "fix" the mirror. I couldn't imagine what she meant until I saw it. It was like looking at a fun house mirror—all wavy and out of proportion. It almost made me queasy! Her bargain purchase had resulted in a great frame with a defective glass. The only way to fix it was to replace the glass.

MIRRORS CAN WORK MAGIC

Mirrors can be beautiful with their silvery color and reflective powers. Just as my sister's *special* mirror was able to mask her weight problem, mirrors can truly work magic in a room by masking problems such as inadequate space or poor light. They are also great for making more of a great view by reflecting it into a room. By placing a mirror opposite a window, you can give the illusion of two windows while simultaneously bringing the outdoors in. For one client I placed a large full-length, arched-top mirror at the top of the stairs. It immediately opened up the space and gave the impression of an archway in what had been a dead end.

In our private spaces, mirrors are practical and necessary. They let us check our hair or makeup. However, in the public spaces of your home, Jane Dupuy of *Southern Accents* magazine says, "[Mirrors] are about definition and decoration rather than checking one's reflection."[1] We always have a choice of using artwork or a mirror. A mirror is an easy choice, especially with a beautiful frame. If you hang a mirror opposite a piece of artwork you can get the best of both worlds—a mirror and a beautiful reflection of artwork!

Here are some easy tips for decorating with mirrors:

- ❧ When hanging a mirror above a fireplace mantel, check the reflection. You don't want the only thing you see to be the ceiling!

- ❧ If a mirror has an incredibly great frame, consider it artwork rather than a frame and worry less about the reflection and more about the placement of the mirror as artwork.

- ❧ Most mirrors have two hooks on the back for hanging. Don't fix a wire from one hook to the other. Instead, use two hangers; your mirror will stay straight. Wire can stretch. It is also easier for the mirror to move and hang crooked from a wire.

- ❧ Color appears stronger in a mirror. Therefore, be sure to consider adjacent color when hanging a mirror. Darker colors can get darker, making a space appear dull, while whites and brighter colors sparkle and create a lighter reflection.

- ❧ When hanging a mirror above a table or counter, be sure to eliminate clutter. You don't want to highlight it.

- ❧ Be careful when hanging mirrors that will reflect lighting fixtures. Often it can create an unbearable glare!

NOTE

1. Jane Dupuy, "Mirror Mirror," *Southern Accents,* September/ October 2003:90.

Meditations on Organizing a Home Office

1 KINGS 10:24-26

"The whole world sought audience with Solomon to hear the wisdom God had put in his heart. Year after year, everyone who came brought a gift–articles of silver and gold, robes, weapons and spices, and horses and mules. Solomon accumulated chariots and horses; he had fourteen hundred chariots and twelve thousand horses."

Day 1
Sometimes, Lord, I cannot get any work done at home because the whole world is clamoring at my work space. I give my frustrations to You.

Day 2
How did Solomon find time to rule when he had so many visitors?

Day 3
Solomon worked from home–his palace. Like all home office workers, the longer he was on duty, the more stuff he accumulated. Did his guests stumble over his stuff on their way to his throne room or wherever he worked?

Day 4
Lord, help me organize my work space in an efficient manner.

Day 5
Thank You that not everyone who visits me brings a gift. I love presents, but I don't really need them. Let me be thankful for pretty little things and spontaneous kisses.

Day 6
Grant me the wisdom of Solomon that I may work to please You and guide my family in Your ways.

Organizing a Home Office

A home office. Finally, a place that is conducive to the way *you* work. No homogenized, cold, steely commercial interior. No flimsy, cramped, eyebrow-height cubicle. Your home office is going to be warm, cozy, and inviting. And best of all, the music playing in the background will be your favorite kind —no more piped-in elevator music.

Unfortunately, many home office spaces resemble a first apartment with makeshift furniture. In fact, many of us would refuse to work for an employer under the conditions we work in at home. Dark, crowded, disorganized, and inefficient spaces not only aren't conducive to productivity but also make us feel miserable. Most of us will avoid entering a space we don't like.

MAKEOVER IS NOT MADNESS

Choosing the right location for your home office is one of the most important aspects to having an effective home office. If, for example, you require quiet, as I do, then consider a remote location. My office is in the basement. My husband's office is on the second floor. That way we can both work from home without disturbing each other. Privacy and the ability to close the door are often overlooked features to a home office.

Once you determine the location, it's time to choose the equipment. Equipment is defined as furniture, files, organizers, fax table or stand, copier, computer, and other items. The most important piece of office equipment is an ergonomically correct chair. If you spend a lot of time at your computer, you need a great chair.

Despite what your mother said, sitting up straight is not good for you. Recent data proves that sitting with your body at 90-degree angles all day is not the healthiest position. In fact, *reclining* is best. As renowned industrial designer Niels Diffrient once said, "The more you recline, the more comfortable you get. Ergo, the best chair is a bed." A great chair lets you sit back in a relaxed position, ears over shoulders, with elbows supported and arms easily stretched forward as you work at your computer.

Organizing and keeping a home office clutter free requires the right equipment. Most of us take the time to research and shop for the right computer, but when it comes to the rest of the office, we use what we have or go buy what's available at a good (cheap) price from the local discount office supply store. I'm warning you; your productivity and happiness will decrease if your office equipment isn't right for your duties or for the space.

If you share your home office space with other family members, designate specific areas for each person and his or her stuff. Be sure to provide enough storage so that your desktop can be clear enough to work. Use the vertical space in your office by purchasing wall-mounted file organizers, shelving, and hanging drawers and cabinets.

SAFETY FIRST

Beyond great equipment, many people overlook safety. Here are some hazards to avoid when planning your workspace:

- Before plugging in any equipment, hire a professional to check whether your home wiring can handle it. Place your desk as close to the electrical outlet as possible. This will keep cords safely out of the way.

- Make sure work surfaces can easily accommodate the weight of your heavy computer. File cabinets should be attached to the wall with a simple L-shaped bracket to keep them from toppling over.

- Eliminate anything that could possibly cause someone to fall; for example, throw rugs, piles of files, or other items left on the floor.

- Working from home often means you finally get a room with a view—a window! Unfortunately, a view can bring an unforeseen problem—a glare on your computer. If moving your desk to a nonglare position is not possible, consider investing in a good window shade or blind or nonglare protector for your screen.

- Lighting a home office area presents its own challenges. Downlights (ceiling spots), compact fluorescent lights, or incandescent fixtures are recommended. Be sure to have a glare-free desktop task light as well.

Meditations on Storage Systems

PROVERBS 21:20

"In the house of the wise are stores of choice food and oil, but a foolish man devours all he has."

Day 1
Is mine a house of the wise?

Day 2
If God took inventory of the items stored in my home, what would He think?

Day 3
How can I be wiser about my purchases and the way I store them?

Day 4
What should I do about storing life's extras?

Day 5
How am I preparing for the future?

Day 6
Am I pleasing the Lord in what I do and say and, thus, stocking provisions in heaven?

Storage Systems

"The wise woman hides the chocolate," Deb says, "but the foolish woman lets her family devour all she has."

You could say Deb has her priorities straight. My mother did too. She was the absolute best at hiding the goodies! What made her so good is that she hid things right in front of our eyes. The chocolate was in the fridge! I still don't know how we didn't find it. I've also heard of mothers hiding goodies in the freezer. Once teenage sons discover that a freezer doubles as a treasure chest, no amount of pleading keeps food from being pirated away. The only thing to do in that case is to bring in more provisions.

STUFF EXPANDS TO FILL THE SPACE ALLOTTED

Now that I've stirred your cravings for chocolate and food, let's get to the facts of life. No matter how much space you are given, you will fill it! The bigger your closet, the more you will put into it. When it comes to storage, two culprits create the problem. First, we are a society of consumptionists who love to save money. To use the coupon for the discount you must purchase three, five, or ten of the same item! Once we've spent good money on something, even if we aren't using it, most of us have a hard time throwing it out. Second, the thought of cleaning, sorting, organizing, and maintaining our wares is something that we all dread and have no time to do. Even if we have time, we don't have a place to put things.

So what's the solution? Wall storage units! Last year I worked on a project for a client who thought her whole life needed reorganizing. Turns out, her garage just needed taming. Her three-car garage floor was covered with so much stuff—some useful, some not—that not even one car fit inside. When we organized it, she felt less chaos and more peaceful about her life. I found a great system for organizing garages called GarageTek. Although originally designed for garages, this storage system works great in many rooms.

USE ALL THE WALL SPACE

A successful storage system utilizes wall space from floor to ceiling, offering endless organizational opportunities. GarageTek starts with PVC-slotted wall panels that are incredibly strong and won't warp or rot. Then you add your choice of innovative modular units and accessories ranging from cabinets and shelving to multifunctional and function-specific storage racks. Best of all, you can reconfigure and expand this system to meet your changing needs.

The key to being spiritually wise is to stock spiritual treasure in heaven. Wouldn't it be great if we were so wise that God had to use wall storage for our spiritual provisions!

Here are a few more ideas for the choice items that you want to store:

> ⚭ When your children receive many gifts at one time, let them enjoy opening them and playing with them for the day. Then hide several items in the attic for a rainy day. (My mom always did this.)

◌ Kids fear closets! They fear the monster that will spring out and get them and things that will fall down and hit them. Even the best-intentioned, most responsible kids can't keep their stuff organized in a closet unless the door opens and shuts easily. Be sure your child's closet door operates properly and has nothing acting as a barrier.

◌ Kids grow fast, and their interests change as they age. Regularly remove everything and sort through it, removing clothing that's too small and toys that are not used.

◌ Adults' interests and hobbies change, too, so don't forget to give away or sell seldom-used hobby equipment. Your friends and neighbors might love that weaving loom or model shipbuilding kit.

◌ Avoid stacking clothing. If you do, someone always wants the slacks from the bottom of the pile and the whole pile goes down!

◌ De-clutter your refrigerator door. Too often it becomes an eyesore and a source of spills. Remove everything. Give the door a good cleaning. Sort through the stuff. Toss what ought to be tossed. Locate a better place for all that you can before repositioning what must be kept on the door.

◌ Get the same container with a different name for a lower price. Instead of purchasing a plastic children's toy chest, check out the sturdy covered plastic boxes in the automotive department. Instead of purchasing clear glass canisters, try using the large glass or plastic jars from the local school cafeteria.

Meditations on Viewing Your Blessings

PSALM 48:12-14

"Walk about Zion, go around her, count her towers, consider well her ramparts, view her citadels, that you may tell of them to the next generation. For this God is our God for ever and ever; he will be our guide even to the end."

Day 1
I praise You, Lord, because all I have comes from You.

Day 2
You are great and worthy of praise.

Day 3
When I walk around my house, view my "citadels," and count my blessings, I can do nothing but bow before You in humble thanksgiving.

Day 4
Help me to tell of Your blessings to the next generation.

Day 5
Let me make Your works plain so future generations can see them and praise You.

Day 6
Be my God forever, and be the God of my children's children.

See photo #4

Viewing Your Blessings

While studying interior design in Venice, Italy, I had the opportunity to see the Doge's Palace. With facades that date from 1309 to 1424 and delicate arcade columns and capitals, it is celebrated for its unique design that can only be termed *Venetian Gothic*. As people walk through the palace, they whisper because they are in awe of this amazing building. I can only imagine the beauty of Zion, but someday I'll walk there too.

Have you noticed how we instinctively walk more slowly and talk more softly when we are in the presence of beauty? These are places that are set apart to be respected and remembered, so we treat them as such.

CITADELS OF LOVE

Take a mental walk around your childhood home. What do you remember? The tire swing your dad hung in the backyard oak? A battered doorframe filled with notches indicating your growth and that of your siblings? Your grandmother's china doll on the mantle that you were allowed to hold once a year?

This week take a walk around your home. What do you count as your citadels of love? What kind of tangible memories are you making for your loved ones? If you aren't sure, you might ask them what places or things in your home are special to them. Or you can start now to create a special place to hold family treasures.

CHERISHED HISTORY

I love a home that tells the story of those that live there. Some mothers fill their Christmas trees with homemade ornaments from their children, and they continue to use the same ornaments year after year. Another family collects Indian arrowheads during vacations and displays them in their home as reminders of their good times. I love to see a family's history displayed in photos. Photos say, "These people are important to us. We care about them. We remember them."

Interior designers can help you choose the perfect sofa or chair, but they cannot buy that special uniqueness that only family treasures can add. A home that incorporates life's treasures makes the ordinary elements extraordinary. Throughout your home include tangible reminders of events that mark milestones for family members. Make them part of the interior decoration. It is a way of celebrating life and finding contentment and appreciation for life's little blessings.

Think how your children's faces will light up when they see their important accomplishments hanging as treasures. Having a special place for these mementos automatically increases the perceived value of the items in that place. Everyone will know that you cherish those things.

CREATE A MEMORY WALL

To create a family history museum, consider choosing one wall on which to hang your favorite photos. My home has a lot of color, so I chose red frames for my photo wall, which is in the hallway between the kitchen and dining room. When friends or family visit, they love to see what new photos have been added. Of course, since I don't have children, my two cats get prominent places. Miss Peony, our Persian/Himalayan cat, is photographed with a vase of pink baby roses. If the facts were known, before the photo was taken she was nibbling on the baby's breath that was delicately placed among the roses—and that's one of our family memories.

Here's some inspiration for starting your memory wall:

- Use crisp white mats with identical frames to give generations of family photos a cohesive feel.

- If you have a combination of black-and-white as well as sepia (brownish-gray to dark olive-brown color) prints, use black frames for a timeless look.

- Don't mix black-and-white photos with color photos. Instead, convert color pictures to black and white.

- Photo labs can enlarge, reduce, and convert photos from negatives or actual prints.

- Use acid-free, four-ply mats to preserve your photos and keep them from sticking to the glass.

- Mats should be 1/8 inch smaller than the photo.

- Don't frame original, old photos. Have copies made and safely store the originals.

- Create a family baby gallery. Gather baby pictures of every family member from newborns to great-grandma. This is a great and fun way to see family resemblances!

- Lay photos out on the floor or a table as you decide how to arrange them. Then transfer each photo to the wall starting at the upper left-hand corner.

Meditations on Blessing Your Home

NUMBERS 6:24–26

"The LORD bless you and keep you; the LORD make his face shine upon you and be gracious to you; the LORD turn his face toward you and give you peace."

Day 1
Blessing is God's idea. Praise the Lord that I don't have to beg for His favor.

Day 2
I love how the words of this blessing flow. Their poetic nature reminds me that God is the author of creativity and beautiful phrases.

Day 3
Thank You, Lord, for Your promise to keep me.

Day 4
Thank You for Your presence that enfolds me in Your grace. I don't have to fear Your wrath.

Day 5
Thank You for Your promise to give peace, not just the lack of strife.

Day 6
How can I bless those around me today and in the following year?

Blessing Your Home

Every summer when I was a child, the priest dropped by our house to bless it. My friends came running and shouting, "The priest is at your house! The priest is at your house!" As a child, I was amazed that the priest would come all the way to my house, walk through each room, and pray a blessing over our humble dwelling.

All of us children gathered at the porch stairs and waited for the priest to come out of the house. We stood there in summer sunsuits, exposing bare legs. We felt vulnerable and awkward being out of school uniforms; nevertheless, we waited. Then we were rewarded. One by one, he laid his hand upon our heads and prayed a blessing over us.

I don't remember what he said, but perhaps he used the familiar words in Numbers. This simple act made us feel special. After receiving the priest's blessings, I felt safe, secure, and confident that God was among us. I felt that our home was connected to our church and God. It meant a lot that the priest would come to pray over us in our personal dwellings. It was truly an awesome event.

REVIVE AN OLD TRADITION

Orthodox Christians for centuries have blessed new dwellings before or just after settling in. Why not extend this tradition to your home, apartment, business, office, or even college dorm room? The simple service of consecration with holy water, oils, and incense is symbolic of the cleansing water of baptism. By setting apart our homes to be places that God is pleased to dwell, we ask for God's grace and presence in our daily lives. This surrendering of our spaces leads us to spiritual associations and awareness in all the places we go, not just the church.

SHOW LOVE WITH BLESSINGS

A blessing is a way of asking God for divine favor to rest upon us. The ancient blessing regarding the tabernacle and the priests who worked there helps us understand the purpose of a blessing: to convey hope that God will have favor on us, be pleased with us, be gracious and merciful toward us, give His approval, and give us peace. By offering a blessing we are showing love and encouraging those who receive it to live faithful lives.

My family has always blessed each home before moving in. We pray at each room's doorway, anointing it with oil in the sign of the cross. As children, such blessings reminded us that God cared about who we were and where we lived. We have reminded ourselves of these blessings after a tragic event within our family.

My mother is Polish, and the traditions that come with her heritage include blessings for everything—even food and pets. I remember carting our Easter meal to the church the day before, for a special blessing. These were memorable occasions for me. If your church doesn't have a special blessing for the home, consider inviting your pastor to visit your home and pray a blessing over it. Celebrate afterward with a meal or dessert.

The Scriptures remind us to begin whatever we do with prayer. So why not bless your home at the beginning of each year?

Here are some ideas for your home blessing:

- Allow the children to lead the pastor around the house with a lit candle.

- Pray that God will have mercy on your house, ridding it of all evil and filling it with His protection and blessing.

- Pray that your home will be filled with the fullness of God and His presence.

- Pray that God will be glorified in every activity that takes place in your home this year.

- Pray for each family member to stand firm in the Lord.

- Ask the Lord to make each family member's love increase and overflow toward Him, one another, and everyone else.

- Pray that all who enter your home may feel the presence of God. Selah! Amen!

Index

NORTHFIELD
P U B L I S H I N G

We hope you enjoyed this product from
Northfield Publishing. Our goal at Northfield
is to provide high quality, thought provoking
and practical books and products that connect
truth to the real needs and challenges of
people like you living in our rapidly changing
world. For more information on other books
and products written and produced from a
biblical perspective write to:

Northfield Publishing
215 West Locust Street
Chicago, IL 60610

<u>BEAUTIFUL PLACES, SPIRITUAL SPACES TEAM</u>

ACQUIRING EDITOR
Elsa Mazon

COPY EDITOR
Ali Childers

COVER DESIGN
Ragont Design

INTERIOR DESIGN
Ragont Design

PRINTING AND BINDING
Color House Graphics

The typeface for the text of this book is
Giovanni